the Language of Song

Selected and edited by
Nicola-Jane Kemp and Heidi Pegler

D1501354

FABER *ff* MUSIC

CONTENTS

HOW TO USE THIS BOOK

The Language of Song series was devised especially for the student singer as an introduction to a wealth of classical song repertoire, and to give them the tools and confidence required to sing in the primary mainland European languages. For this reason, no sung English translations are provided. The songs have been carefully chosen for their appropriateness of text and vocal range for the young student singer.

Preface to each song

Each song or aria is prefaced by a page of notes, containing: a brief background (setting it in its historical context or, where appropriate, its place in the drama); an idiomatic translation; and a phonetic pronunciation of the text. Any further notes at the bottom of each page highlight particular language points that may arise in the individual texts.

Translations: There are two translations for each song or aria. The first is a word-for-word translation directly underneath the text in the musical score. This is to enable the student to see exactly which words will be important for emphasis and interpretation. In addition, the prefatory page to each song includes an idiomatic translation, which will clarify the meaning of the text in grammatical English.

Phonetic pronunciation: A phonetic pronunciation of the original language, using the International Phonetic Alphabet (IPA), is provided for each song. A key to pronunciation is provided for each language at the back of this book and includes both examples from the song texts together with the closest English equivalents to the sounds explained. IPA symbols are given in these guides and careful study of these pages will be required in order to fully understand the IPA symbols that accompany the text for each song or aria. These are some of the basic principles that will help the singer to work along the right lines until they are able to refine pronunciation further with the help of a specialist language coach.

The accompanying CDs

The CDs provide the text for each song or aria spoken by the language consultants, all of whom are native speakers and work regularly with professional singers (see Biographies below). The speakers have attempted to make the text as clear as possible whilst maintaining the overall flow and dramatic content of the language. It is recommended that the language texts are prepared independently from the musical melody at first, as follows:

- Read the pronunciation key for the relevant language.
- Listen to the text on the CD, following the IPA guide for the song.
- Practise speaking the text slowly and clearly.
- When confident, slowly speak the text in the rhythm of the music.
- Gradually increase your speed to match the speed of the song.
- Additionally, practise delivering the text as a dramatic recitation showing your understanding of the language.

The CDs also include backing accompaniments for each song or aria. It should be remembered that these are a practice aid only and should not be substituted for a live accompaniment in performance.

Wherever possible, every effort has been made to return to the original source material. New accompaniments have been arranged for the Arie Antique and some (optional) ornamentation suggested, which appears in small staff notation above the vocal line. Editorial additions, such as dynamics, appear in square brackets.

EDITORS & CONSULTANTS: BIOGRAPHIES

Nicola-Jane Kemp

Nicola-Jane is a professional singer, specialising in the coloratura repertoire (her signature role is 'Queen of the Night'), and works for companies as diverse as Music Theatre Wales and the Festival Lyrique d'Aix-en-Provence, France. She has been broadcast on BBC Radio and her concert work takes her all over the UK – including the South Bank, the Barbican, St Martin-in-the-Fields and St John's, Smith Square in London – and to the Middle East. She is an examiner for the Associated Board of the Royal Schools of Music and currently teaches voice to choral scholars at Clare and Queens' Colleges in Cambridge, and at St Paul's Girls' School, Hammersmith, London.

Heidi Pegler

Heidi is Head of Singing at St Paul's Girls' School in London, where she runs a lively and busy singing department. She is an examiner for the Associated Board of the Royal Schools of Music. She was a contributor to both *A Common Approach 2002* and *All Together!* – a book focusing on teaching music in groups (ABRSM). As a professional singer, she specialises in Baroque music (her debut solo CD, *Hark! the echoing air*, features Baroque music for Soprano, Trumpet and Orchestra) and has performed at many of Britain's leading venues including the Royal Albert Hall in London, St David's Hall, Cardiff and the Royal Concert Hall, Glasgow.

Tina Ruta (Italian Consultant)

Born in Naples, Tina studied there at the Conservatoire San Pietro a Maiella and continued her studies with Mark Raphael and Herbert-Caesari in England. As a singer, she has performed in operas and recitals in England, France and Italy and has appeared in London's West End, at Glyndebourne, and in television plays. She has since gone on to develop a highly sought-after practice as an Italian language coach and has taught at the Guildhall School of Music and Drama and Trinity College of Music, both of which awarded her fellowships. She has also coached singers at Covent Garden, Le Châtelet, Opera-Bastille, La Monnaie, Brussels, Berlin State Opera, Vienna State Opera and Volksoper, Bavarian State Opera, Helsinki Opera House, the Sibelius and Amsterdam conservatoires, and for record labels Phillips, Decca, Deutsche Grammophon and EMI. In the course of her work, Tina has collaborated with many conductors, including Giulini, Muti, Sinopoli, Colin Davis, Myung Whun Chung and Pappano. She also translates film scripts, librettos and lyrics.

Franziska Roth (German Consultant)

Franziska was born and grew up in Germany. She studied musicology at Salzburg University, and continued her studies in piano and singing at the 'Mozarteum' Academy of Music. She has worked as a language coach for opera productions at Covent Garden, Glyndebourne, Le Châtelet and Opera-Bastille in Paris; festivals in Aix-en-Provence and Salzburg, and for staged projects in Carnegie Hall, New York. She is highly sought after by many of the world's leading singers as a Lieder and oratorio coach, and has worked for many great conductors, including Barenboim, Rattle, Solti, Haitink, Ghergiev, Pappano, Gardiner and Thielemann. She is also regularly employed by the major recording companies, including EMI, Deutsche Grammophon, Decca, Sony and Chandos. She has been a member of the teaching staff at the Royal College of Music, London since 1989.

Michel Vallat (French Consultant)

Michel Vallat was born in France. He studied at the Sorbonne in Paris, where he graduated with a degree in Philosophy, and at the Conservatoire National Superieur de Musique de Paris, where he won both the *Premier Prix de chant* and the *Premier Prix d'Art lyrique*. Michel undertook further studies in French mélodie with Gerard Souzay, and also studied in Italy with Maestro Valdomiro Badiali and Carlo Bergonzi. He was later appointed French coach at the Royal College of Music and Professor of Singing at the Guildhall School of Music and Drama, London. He works regularly with Welsh National Opera, Scottish Opera, the Glyndebourne Festival and the Royal Opera House (Covent Garden), and with singers such as Valerie Masterson, Della Jones, Thomas Hampson, Sergiev Leeferkus, Bruce Ford, Renée Fleming, David Daniels, Sally Matthews, Joseph Calleja, Angelika Kirchschlager and Christopher Maltman.

Ludmilla Andrew (Russian Consultant)

Ludmilla was born in Canada of Russian parentage and has enjoyed a distinguished international career with the world's leading operas companies, including San Francisco Opera and New York's Metropolitan Opera. She has sung many of the great dramatic soprano title roles, including *Madame Butterfly*, *Tosca*, *Turandot*, *Aida*, *Lady Macbeth*, *Anna Bolena* and *Norma*. She has also specialised in Russian repertoire, with a recital of Russian songs by Nicolai Medtner included amongst her many recordings. She is now one of Britain's leading vocal coaches, working with many young singers, and is frequently invited to sit on competition and opera casting panels. She is the Russian coach at the Royal Academy of Music, London and also vocal and language coach for Chandos Records.

The Editors wish to thank the following for their invaluable contribution to the production of this book: Richard Shaw for advice on Russian; Coral Johnson for Italian manuscripts; Nigel Foster for repertoire advice and general assistance; and St Paul's Girls' School for the generous use of its premises during the CD recording.

© 2008 by Faber Music Ltd
This corrected edition first published in 2011
Bloomsbury House 74–77 Great Russell Street London WC1B 3DA
Cover design by Økvik Design
Music processed by MusicSet 2000
Additional processing by Ashley Harries
Printed in England by Caligraving Ltd
All rights reserved

ISBN10: 0-571-53075-3
EAN13: 978-0-571-53075-5

To buy Faber Music publications or to find out about the full range of titles available
please contact your local music retailer or Faber Music sales enquiries:

Faber Music Limited, Burnt Mill, Elizabeth Way, Harlow, CM20 2HX England
Tel: +44 (0)1279 82 89 82   Fax: +44 (0)1279 82 89 83
sales@fabermusic.com   fabermusic.com

CDs recorded at St Paul's Girls' School, Hammersmith, London, June 2008
Piano: Iain Farrington; Language consultants: Tina Ruta, Franziska Roth, Michel Vallat, Ludmilla Andrew
Recorded by Mike Skeet; Produced by Nicola-Jane Kemp and Heidi Pegler
℗ & © 2008 Faber Music Ltd

Pur dicesti, o bocca bella

O beautiful mouth   Antonio Lotti (1667–1740)

Background

Antonio Lotti studied under Giovanni Legrenzi and joined the choir of St Mark's Basilica in Venice where he sang as an alto. He went on to work there in various capacities throughout his life, finally becoming Maestro di Cappella in 1736 until his death. Lotti's music bridges the Baroque and burgeoning Classical styles. He composed in several different genres, including sacred motets (his 'Miserere' is sung in St Mark's to this day), masses and cantatas, madrigals and some thirty operas. Renowned as a teacher, his students included Marcello, Alberti, Bassani, Gasparini, and Galuppi. This aria comes from Act Two of the opera *Arminius* and Auguste Gevaert published it in his collection *Les Gloires de l'Italie* (Paris 1868). Parisotti also included it in his collection of *Arie Antiche* in 1890.

Idiomatic translation

O beautiful lips, you did say that dear, gentle "yes",
which makes my joy complete.
Honouring his flame,
Love opened you, the sweet fountain of delight, with a kiss.

Pronunciation – **Pur dicesti, o bocca bella** [pur ditʃesti o bɔk:ka bɛl:la]

Pur dicesti, o bocca bella,
pur ditʃesti o bɔk:ka bɛl:la

quel soave e caro sì,
kwel soave karɔ si

che fa tutto il mio piacer.
ke fa tut:tɔil mio pjatʃer

Per onor di sua facella
per ɔnor di sua fatʃel:la

con un bacio Amor t'aprì,
kɔn un batʃɔamor tapri

dolce fonte del goder.
dɔltʃe fɔnte del goder

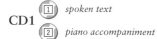

CD1 · spoken text
· piano accompaniment

Pur dicesti, o bocca bella
O beautiful mouth

Anonymous

Antonio Lotti
(1667–1740)
arr. Heidi Pegler

54

mio pia - cer,_____ il mio pia - cer,

mio pia - cer,_____ il mio pia - cer,
my pleasure, [the] my pleasure,

61 [mp] [mf]

quel so - a - ve e___ ca - ro___ sì, si,___ che___ fa tut - to il

quel so - a - ve e___ ca - ro___ sì, sì,___ che___ fa tut - to il
that gentle and dear yes, yes, which makes all [the]

67

mio pia - cer,_____ il mio pia - cer.

mio pia - cer,_____ il mio pia - cer.
my pleasure, [the] my pleasure.

74 FINE

[mf]

O del mio dolce ardor bramato oggetto

O desired object of my sweet ardour   Christoph Gluck (1714–87)

Background

Gluck, the son of a forester, was born in Erasbach (then in Czechoslovakia but now in German Bavaria). His passion for music led him to break from his family and travel to pursue his gifts – he studied in Prague and Vienna, and then found his way to Milan and began to compose Italian operas in the *opera seria* and *opera buffa* styles. He finally settled in Vienna, where he became Kapellmeister at the Hapsburg court. As his fame spread, he worked with a young Marie Antoinette in Paris, who became a patron of his. Gluck wrote several French operas in the *opera comique* style. He is, however, best remembered for beginning to challenge the prevailing operatic conventions of the time and developing a more natural dramatic style that was to influence many later composers. The first significant opera in this style was *Orfeo ed Euridice*, performed in Vienna in 1762, followed later by *Paride ed Elena* in 1770 from which this aria comes. In the story from Homer's *Iliad*, Paris was asked to judge which of three goddesses was the most beautiful. His reward for selecting Aphrodite, the goddess of love, was to gain the love of the most beautiful woman in the world – Helen. This song appears at the opening of the opera as Paris arrives on a beach near Sparta and is full of happy anticipation at finally seeing the woman promised to him.

Idiomatic translation

O desired object of my sweet ardour,
at last, the air which you breathe, I breathe.
Wherever I turn my glance, love paints your lovely features in my mind.
My thoughts imagine the most happy hopes,
and in the longing which fills my breast,
I seek you, I call you, I hope and I sigh.

Pronunciation – O del mio dolce ardor bramato oggetto [ɔ dɛl miɔ dɔltʃeardor bramatodːʒetːɔ]

O del mio dolce͜ardor
ɔ dɛl miɔ dɔltʃeardor

bramato͜oggetto,
bramatodːʒetːɔ

l'aura che tu respiri,
laura ke tu respiri

alfin respiro.
alfin respirɔ

Ovunque il guardo io giro,
ɔvunkwe il gwardɔiɔ dʒirɔ

le tue vaghe sembianze
le tue vage sembjantse

amore͜in me dipinge:
amɔrein me dipindʒe

Il mio pensier si finge
il miɔ pensjɛr si findʒe

le più liete speranze,
le pju ljɛte sperantse

e nel desio che così
e nɛl deziɔ kɛ kozi

m'empie il petto,
mɛmpje il petːɔ

cerco te, chiamo te, spero e sospiro.
tʃɛrkɔ te, kjamɔ te, sperɔ e sɔspirɔ

Further notes

Take care to pronounce every *n* with the tip of the tongue behind the top teeth. An English **ng** as in 'song' [sɔŋ] would not be correct for words such as **finge** or **dipinge** (see the key to Italian pronunciation at the back of this volume).

O del mio dolce ardor bramato oggetto

O desired object of my sweet ardour

Raniero de' Calzabigi
(1714–95)

Christoph von Gluck
(1714–87)
arr. Heidi Pegler

14

* Recording cue

* Recording cue

La conocchia

The flax spinner

Gaetano Donizetti (1797–1848)

from *Nuits d'été à Pausilippe* No. 5

Background

Donizetti was born into a poor and unmusical family in Bergamo, Italy. Musical training in his home town, however, led him to compose operas and he soon found himself with a contract in Naples. His international reputation was finally secured in 1830 with the success of *Anna Bolena,* which was premiered in Milan. Other comic operas were to follow, including *L'Elisir d'amore* and *Don Pasquale*, but his most famous opera is probably the tragedy *Lucia di Lammermoor*, written in 1835 and considered one of the best examples of the *bel canto* tradition. Donizetti is primarily remembered for his operas (around seventy altogether) but he also composed in other genres, including nearly two hundred songs. Written in a Neapolitan dialect, this song is dedicated to the Neapolitan bass Luigi Lablache and comes from the song cycle *Nuits d'été à Pausilippe* ('Summer nights at Pausilippe'). Donizetti's family was destined for tragedy: all of his children died young, his wife died of cholera, and he himself descended into mental illness (possibly resulting from syphilis) and spent his final years in mental institutions in Paris and Bergamo.

Idiomatic translation

When I want to speak to my sweetheart,
for I often feel the desire,
I sit at my window and spin,
when I want to speak to my sweetheart.

When he comes past, I break off the thread,
and charmingly ask,
"sweetheart, please throw it back to me,"
and as he picks it up, I just look at him.
And thus I continue to thread and thread – alas!

Pronunciation – **La conocchia** [la kɔnɔkja]

Quann'a lo bello mio voglio parlare,

kwan:na lɔ bɛl:lɔ miɔ vɔʎɔ parlare

ca spisso me ne vene lu golio,

ka ʃpis:sɔ me nɛ vene lu gɔliɔ

a la fenesta me mett'a filare,

a la fenesta me met:ta filare

quann'a lo bello mio voglio parlare.

kwan:na lɔ bɛl:lɔ miɔ vɔʎɔ parlare

Quann'isso passa, po' rompo lo filo

kwan:nis:sɔ pas:sa po rompo lɔ filɔ

e con 'na grazia me mett'a priare,

e kɔn na gratsja me met:ta priare

bello, peccarità, proitemillo,

bɛl:lɔ pɛk:karita proitemil:lɔ

isso lu piglia, e io lo sto a guardare,

is:sɔ lu piʎa e iɔ lɔ stɔa gwardare

e accossì me ne vao' mpilo mpilo, ajemè!

eakɔs:si me nɛ vaɔ mpilɔ mpilɔ aime

Further notes

This song is written in a Neapolitan dialect, and the phonetics and recording provide a more italianate pronunciation. Check the phonetics and listen carefully to the CD. In the word **ajemè** the *j* is equivalent to a modern [i].

La conocchia

The flax spinner

CD1 ⑤ *spoken text*
⑥ *piano accompaniment*

Neapolitan Song

Gaetano Donizetti
(1797–1848)

Moderato mosso ♩. = 76

Original key

Quan-n'a lo bel - lo mio vo-glio par-la - re, ca spis-so me ne
When to the handsome-one my I-want to—speak, as often to—me of—it

ve-ne lu go-li - o, a la fe-ne-sta me mett'a fi -
comes the desire, at the window myself place to—

-la - re, quann' a lo bel - lo mio vo-glio par-la -
-spin, when to the handsome—one my I want to—speak.

* Recording cue

Per pietà, bell'idol mio

For pity's sake, my beloved

Vincenzo Bellini (1801–35)

from *Sei Ariette* No. 5

Background

Born in Sicily, Bellini's musical gift shone through from an early age. He studied in Naples and went on to become one of the foremost composers of the *bel canto* operatic style in the 19th century. This style embodied superlative vocal technique where a seamless quality of line was required, combined with great expressive abilites and formidable agility. In his short life he made a lasting contribution to the world of opera and is particularly remembered for *Norma, Capuletti e I Montecchi* and *I Puritani*, three of the greatest works in the repertoire. In addition he wrote a number of pieces for voice and piano that brought his highly expressive and rather melancholic style into the private drawing-room. This song was written in 1829 and was published by Ricordi as part of his *Composizione da camera per canto e pianoforte* in 1938.

Idiomatic translation

For pity's sake, my beautiful loved one,
do not say to me that I am ungrateful;
Heaven has made me wretched and unfortunate enough.

If I am faithful to you,
if I pine for your beautiful eyes,
Love knows, the gods know,
my heart and yours knows.

Pronunciation – Per pietà, bell'idol mio [pɛr pjeta bɛl:lidol mɔ]

Per pietà, bell'idol mio
pɛr pjeta bɛl:lidol mɔ

Non mi dir ch'io sono ingrato;
nɔn mi dir kiɔ sɔnɔ ingratɔ

Infelice e sventurato
infelitʃe zvɛnturatɔ

Abbastanza il ciel mi fa.
ab:bastantsail tʃel mi fa

Se fedele a te son io
sɛ fedele a te sɔn iɔ

Se mi struggo ai tuoi bei lumi,
sɛ mi strug:gɔ ai twɔi bɛi lumi

Sallo amor lo sanno i Numi,
sal:lɔamɔr lɔ san:nɔi numi

Il mio core, il tuo lo sa.
il miɔ kɔre il tuɔ lɔ sa

Further notes

Note the voiced *s* in **sventurato** [zvɛnturatɔ].

Per pietà, bell'idol mio

For pity's sake, my beloved

CD1 · spoken text · piano accompaniment

Pietro Metastasio
(1698–1782)

Vincenzo Bellini
(1801–35)

* Recording cue

* Recording cue

La pastorella delle Alpi

The shepherdess of the Alps

Gioachino Rossini (1792–1868)

Background

Rossini was born in Pesaro, Italy, to musical parents (his father was a horn player and his mother a singer). In his youth he learned to play the piano, horn and cello, and he also sang. After further general musical studies in Bologna, he won plaudits as a young composer and his first opera was staged when he was only eighteen. His first big success was *Tancredi* in 1813 and he went on to compose nearly forty operas, the most famous of which include *Il Barbiere di Siviglia* (1815), *La Cenerentola* (1817), *L'Italiana in Algeri* (1813) and *Guillaume Tell* (1829). Following this last opera, written in 1829, Rossini seems to have gone into semi-retirement at the age of thirty-seven, and though he continued to write cantatas, instrumental music, and sacred and secular vocal music, his productivity and the public acclamation he enjoyed in his early life was never again equalled. This song comes from the set *Serate Musicali* (Musical Soirées) 1830–35 and aptly represents Rossini's witty and lively musical style.

Idiomatic translation

I am the pretty shepherdess	Whoever in the night's dread
who comes down each morning	has lost the right path,
and offers a little basket	at my hut,
of fresh fruit and flowers.	will find the way again.
Whoever comes at first dawn	Come, o traveller
will have some pretty roses	the shepherdess is here,
and dewy apples.	but the flower of her thoughts
Come to my garden,	will be given to one man alone.
ahu, ahu …	ahu, ahu …

Pronunciation – La pastorella delle Alpi [la pastɔrɛl:la dɛl:le alpi]

Son bella pastorella,	**Chi nel notturno orrore**
son bɛl:la pastɔrɛl:la	ki nel nɔt:turnɔr:rɔre
che scende ogni mattino,	**smarrì la buona via,**
ke ʃende ɔɲi mat:tinɔ	smar:ri la bwɔna via
ed offre un cestellino	**alla capanna mia**
ɛd ɔf:freun tʃestɛl:linɔ	al:la kap:pan:na mia
di fresche frutta e fior.	**ritroverà il cammin.**
di freske frut:tae fjor	ritroverail kam:min
Chi viene al primo albore	**Venite, o passaggiero,**
ki vjeneal primɔalbore	veniteo pas:sad:ʒerɔ
avrà vezzose rose	**la pastorella è qua,**
avra vet:sɔze rɔze	la pastɔrɛl:la ɛ kwa
e poma rugiadose,	**ma il fior del suo pensiero**
e pɔma rudʒadɔze	mail fjor del suɔ pensierɔ
venite al mio giardin. Ahu	**ad uno sol darà! Ahu**
venite al miɔ dʒardin au	ad unɔ sol dara au

Further notes

There are many words with double consonants here. Even at the fast speed of this song, make sure that a slight stop on the consonant is achieved (see the key to Italian pronunciation at the back of this volume).

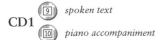

CD1 · spoken text · piano accompaniment

La pastorella delle Alpi
The shepherdess of the Alps

Conte Carlo Pepoli
(1796–1881)

Gioachino Rossini
(1792–1868)

Son bel-la pas-to-rel - la, che scen-de o-gni mat - ti - no,
I—am (the) beautiful shepherdess, who descends each morning,
Chi nel not - tur-no or-ro - re smar-rì la buo-na vi - a,
Whoever in [–the] nocturnal horror has–lost the good path,

ed of-fre un ce-stel-li - no di fre-sche frut-ta e fior.
and offers a little–basket of fresh fruit and flowers.
al-la ca-pan-na mi - a ri-tro-ve-rà il cam - min.
at–the hut mine will–find–again the way.

Mattinata

Morning   **Ruggiero Leoncavallo (1857–1919)**

Background

Ruggiero Leoncavallo was born in Naples. Although his father was a judge, he shunned a career in the law and went into opera as a librettist and composer, studying music at the Conservatorio San Pietro a Majella in Naples and literature at Bologna University. His first big success came with the opera *Pagliacci*, performed in Milan in 1892 and written in the 'verismo' style – a movement that aimed to depict contemporary life, especially the life of the lower classes, in all its violent and sometimes sordid realism. Leoncavallo wrote other operas in his lifetime, but today he is principally remembered for *Pagliacci*, his libretto for Puccini's opera *Manon Lescaut* and this song, recorded by the great tenor Enrico Caruso in 1904.

Idiomatic translation

The dawn, dressed in white,
is opening her door to the great sun,
and with rosy fingers
caresses the multitude of flowers.
All creation appears to be
moved by a mysterious quiver,

yet you will not wake up, and in vain
I stand here sadly and sing.
You also, put on your white dress
and open the door to your singer!
Wherever you are not, light is absent;
wherever you are, love is born!

Pronunciation – **Mattinata** [mat:tinata]

L'aurora, di bianco vestita,
laur<u>o</u>ra   di bj<u>a</u>nkɔ vest<u>i</u>ta

già l'uscio dischiude al gran sol,
ʤa luʃɔ   diskj<u>u</u>deal   gran sol

di già, con le rosee sue dita
di ʤa   kɔn le r<u>o</u>ze   s<u>ue</u> d<u>i</u>ta

carezza de' fiori lo stuol!
kar<u>e</u>t:tsa de fj<u>o</u>ri lo stw<u>ɔ</u>l

Commosso da un fremito arcano
kɔm:m<u>o</u>s:sɔ daun fr<u>e</u>mitɔark<u>a</u>nɔ

intorno il creato già par,
int<u>o</u>rnɔil kre<u>a</u>tɔ ʤa par

e tu non ti desti, ed invano
e tu nɔn ti d<u>ɛ</u>sti ed inv<u>a</u>nɔ

mi sto qui dolente a cantar.
mi stɔ kwi dɔl<u>ɛ</u>ntea kant<u>a</u>r

Metti anche tu la veste bianca
m<u>e</u>t:tianke tu la v<u>ɛ</u>ste bj<u>a</u>nka

e schiudi l'uscio al tuo cantor!
e skj<u>u</u>di luʃɔ   al t<u>uo</u> kant<u>ɔ</u>r

Ove non sei la luce manca,
<u>o</u>ve nɔn s<u>ɛ</u>i la lutʃe m<u>a</u>nka

ove tu sei nasce l'amor!
<u>o</u>ve tu s<u>ɛ</u>i n<u>a</u>ʃe lam<u>o</u>r

Further notes

The consonant combination …**schi** is pronounced [ski]. Take care not to insert the English sound …*ng* into words such as *bianco* or *manca*. The *n* is formed with the tip of the tongue behind the top teeth (see the key to Italian pronunciation at the back of this volume). Note that **desti** (wake up) must be pronounced with an open *e* [ɛ] to avoid confusion with **desti** [desti], which means 'you gave'.

spoken text

piano accompaniment

Mattinata
Morning

Ruggiero Leoncavallo
(1857–1919)

Ruggiero Leoncavallo
(1857–1919)
arr. Heidi Pegler

© 2008 by Faber Music Ltd

tu la ve - ste bian-ca e schiu - di l'u - scio al tuo can -
you the dress white and open the door to your singer!

a tempo con anima

- tor! O - ve non se - i la lu - ce man - ca, o - ve tu
Where not you–are the light lacks, where you

se - i nas - ce l'a - mor!
are is–born the love!

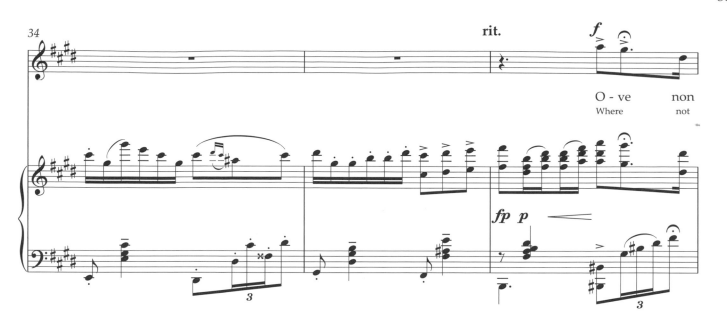

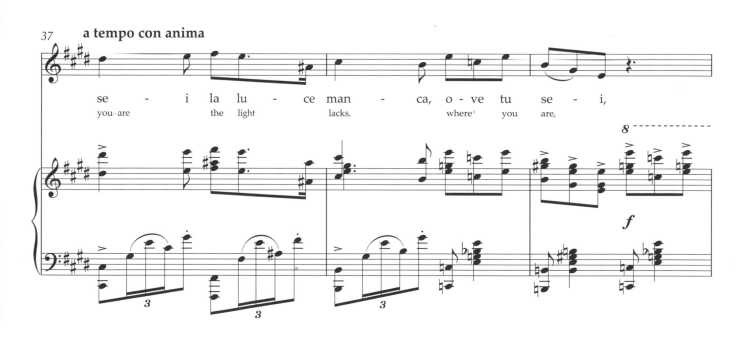

Widmung

Dedication

from *Myrthen*

Robert Schumann (1810–56) Op. 25 No. 1

Background

'Widmung' is the first song in the cycle *Myrthen, Liederkreis* ('Myrtles, Song-cycle'), which comprises twenty-six songs composed by Schumann in February 1840 as a wedding present for his beloved Clara Wieck. The pair were forcibly separated by Clara's father, who opposed their union, and the song-cycle recollects the joy and pain of love, and being apart. The text is taken from a poem by Friedrich Rückert (1788–1866), which conveys the idea of the transforming power of love between a man and a woman. It is one of several themes concerning relationships that Schumann explores throughout the cycle and it also contains some specially hidden ciphers and messages that Schumann and Clara secretly shared between them.

Idiomatic translation

You my soul, you my heart,
you my joy, O you my pain,
you the world in which I live,
you my heaven, in which I float,
O you my grave, into which
I forever lay down my grief.

You are tranquillity, you are peace,
Heaven has bestowed you upon me.
That you love me gives me my worth,
your gaze transfigures me,
you raise me lovingly above myself,
my good spirit, my better self!

Pronunciation – **Widmung** [vɪtmʊŋ]

Du meine Seele, du mein Herz,
duː maɪnə zeːlə duː maɪn hɛrts

du meine Wonn', o du mein Schmerz,
duː maɪnə vɔn |oː duː maɪn ʃmɛrts

du meine Welt, in der ich lebe,
duː maɪnə vɛlt |ɪn deːɐ |ɪç leːbə

mein Himmel du, darein ich schwebe,
maɪn hɪməl duː daraɪn |ɪç ʃveːbə

o du mein Grab, in das hinab
|oː duː maɪn grap |ɪn das hɪnap

ich ewig meinen Kummer gab!
|ɪç |eːvɪç maɪnən kʊmɐ gaːp

Du bist die Ruh', du bist der Frieden,
duː bɪst diː ruː duː bɪst deːɐ friːdən

du bist vom Himmel mir beschieden.
duː bɪst fɔm hɪməl miːɐ bəʃiːdən

Daß du mich liebst, macht mich mir wert,
das duː mɪç liːbst maxt mɪç miːɐ veːrt

dein Blick hat mich vor mir verklärt,
daɪn blɪk hat mɪç foːɐ miːɐ fɐkleːrt

du hebst mich liebend über mich,
duː heːbst mɪç liːbənt |yːbɐ mɪç

mein guter Geist, mein bess'res Ich!
maɪn guːtɐ gaist, maɪn bɛsrəs |ɪç

Widmung
Dedication

CD1 [13] *spoken text*
[14] *piano accompaniment*

Friedrich Rückert
(1788–1866)

Robert Schumann Op. 25 No. 1
(1810–56)

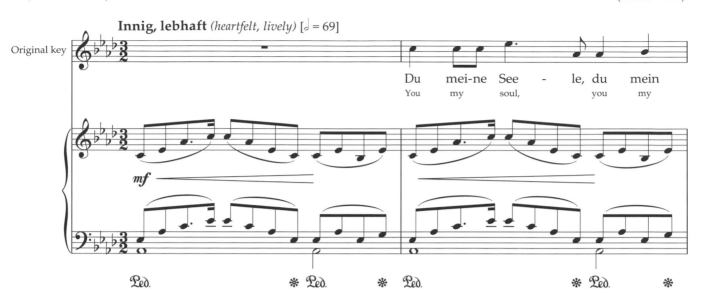

Du mei-ne See - le, du mein
You my soul, you my

Herz, du mei-ne Wonn', o du mein Schmerz, du mei-ne
heart, you my joy, o you my pain, you my

Welt, in der ich le - be, mein Him-mel du, dar-ein ich
world, in which I live, my heaven you, into–it I

steigend und eiland
(increasing and hurrying)

Schmerz, du mei-ne Welt, in der ich le - be, mein Him - mel
pain, you my world, in which I live, my heaven

du, dar - ein ich schwe - be, mein gu - ter Geist, mein bess' - res
you, into—it I float, my good spirit, my better

Ich!
self!

Du bist die Ruh

You are rest   Franz Schubert (1797–1828) Op. 59 No. 3 D776

Background
This song, written in 1823, was published in 1826 as part of a collection entitled *Four Songs by Rückert and Graf Platen*. The text comes from *Östliche Rosen* ('Oriental Roses'), a collection of untitled poems, the name of which Schubert chose himself. He sets this poem in a simple, almost religious expression of selfless love.

Idiomatic translation

You are rest, the gentle peace,
you are longing and what stills it.
I dedicate to you full of joy and pain
as a dwelling here my eyes and heart.

Come in to me, and close
the door quietly behind you.
Drive other pain from this breast!
May my heart be filled with your joy.

This canopy of my eyes is lit up
by your radiance alone. O fill it completely.

Pronunciation – **Du bist die Ruh** [duː bɪst diː ruː]

Du bist die Ruh, der Friede mild,
duː bist diː ruː   deːɐ friːdə mɪlt

die Sehnsucht du, und was sie stillt.
diː zeːnzʊxt duː |ʊnt vas zi ʃtɪlt

Ich weihe dir voll Lust und Schmerz
|ɪç vaːiə diːɐ fɔl lʊst |ʊnt ʃmɛrts

zur Wohnung hier mein Aug und Herz.
tsuːɐ voːnuːŋ   hiːɐ main |auk |ʊnt hɛrts

Kehr ein bei mir, und schließe du
keːr |ain bai miːɐ |ʊnt ʃliːsə   duː

still hinter dir die Pforten zu.
ʃtɪl hɪntɐ diːɐ diː pfɔrtən tsuː

Treib andern Schmerz aus dieser Brust!
traip |andɛrn ʃmɛrts |aus diːzɐ brʊst

Voll sei dies Herz von deiner Lust.
fɔl zai diːs hɛrts fɔn dainɐ lʊst

Dies Augenzelt, von deinem Glanz
diːs |augəntsɛlt fɔn dainəm glants

allein erhellt, o füll es ganz.
|alain |ɛɐhɛlt |oː fʏl |es gants

CD1

spoken text

piano accompaniment

Du bist die Ruh

You are rest

Friedrich Rückert
(1788–1866)

Franz Schubert Op. 59 No. 3 D776
(1797–1828)

Du bist die Ruh, der Frie - de mild, die Sehn - sucht du, und was sie stillt.
You are the calm, the peace mild, the longing you, and what it stills.

Ich wei - he dir_____ voll_ Lust_ und_ Schmerz zur Woh - nung hier_____
I dedicate to–you full (of) joy and pain as–the dwelling here

mein_ Aug_ und_ Herz,_____ mein_ Aug_ und_ Herz._____
my eye and heart, my eye and heart.

Verborgenheit

Seclusion

Hugo Wolf (1860–1903) M12

Background

Hugo Wolf learned the piano and violin as a child, and became a music critic in Vienna at the age of twenty-four. A combination of the effects of syphilis and a bi-polar temperament resulted in difficulties sustaining relationships and regular work. Nevertheless, at twenty-eight he entered a swift (and all too short) period of intense creative activity, composing over two hundred songs between 1888 and 1891. Dying tragically early of syphilitic mental deterioration at the age of forty-three, his final years included brief outbursts of great compositional activity, composing up to three songs in a day at times, and long years of silence in between. He wrote an opera and some instrumental music, but he is primarily remembered for his immense legacy of Lieder. 'Verborgenheit' (1888) comes from a collection of settings by the pastor, artist and poet Eduard Mörike, whose themes explore the heights and depths of everyday life, and in this case, of love's conflicting emotions – something that Wolf himself may have closely identified with.

Idiomatic translation

Let, o world, o let me be!
Do not tempt me with gifts of love,
Leave this heart alone to feel
Its delight, its pain!

I know not why I grieve,
It is unknown woe;
Constantly, through tears
I see the sun's dear light.

Often, I am hardly aware,
And bright joy quivers
Through the heaviness that oppresses me,
Delighting my heart.

Let, o world, etc. …

Pronunciation – **Verborgenheit** [fɛɐbɔrgənhait]

Laß, o Welt, o laß mich sein!
las |oː vɛlt |oː las mɪç zain

Locket nicht mit Liebesgaben,
lɔkət   nɪçt mɪt liːbəsgaːbən

Laßt dies Herz   alleine haben
last diːs hɛrts |alainə haːbən

Seine Wonne, seine Pein!
zainə vɔnə,   zainə pain

Was ich traure, weiß ich nicht,
vas |ɪç traurə vais |ɪç nɪçt

Es ist unbekanntes Wehe;
|ɛs |ɪst |ʊnbəkantəs veːe

Immerdar durch Tränen sehe
|ɪmɐdar   dʊrç* trɛːnən seːə

Ich der Sonne liebes Licht.
|ɪç deːɐ zɔnə liːbəs lɪçt

Oft bin ich mir kaum bewußt,
|ɔft bɪn |ɪç miːɐ kaum bəvʊst

Und die helle Freude zücket
|ʊnt diː hɛlə frɔidə tsʏkət

Durch die Schwere, so mich drücket
dʊrç diː ʃverə   zoː mɪç drʏkət

Wonniglich in meiner Brust.
vɔnɪklɪç |ɪn mainɐ brʊst

Laß, o Welt, …etc
las |oː vɛlt

Further notes

Ensure that the *ch* [ç] sounds are correctly pronounced. They are all the same in this song.
* The word **durch** is problematic for English speakers. Practise saying [dʊr – ɪç], then leave out the [ɪ] – [dʊr – ç], then bring the two sounds closer together. In bar 15 however, the word **durch** is of such short duration that it is better to omit the *r* and replace it with [ɐ], thus pronouncing it [dʊɐç]. Note also that in German, where words ending in *-ig* have the suffix *-lich*, the *g* is hardened to a *k*. For example, **wonniglich** is pronounced [vɔnɪklɪç].

Verborgenheit

Seclusion

Eduard Mörike
(1804–75)

Hugo Wolf M12
(1860–1903)

Mässig und sehr innig
(*Moderate and very heartfelt*) [♩ = 60]

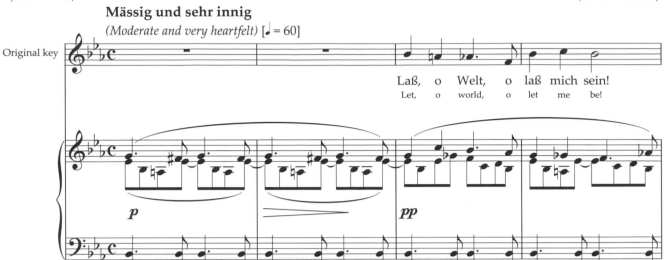

Laß, o Welt, o laß mich sein!
Let, o world, o let me be!

Lo - cket nicht mit Lie - bes - ga - ben, Laßt dies Herz al - lei - ne ha - ben
Tempt (me) not with love's-gifts, let this heart alone to-have

rit.   *a tempo*

Sei - ne Won - ne, sei - ne Pein!   Was ich trau - re, weiß ich nicht,—
its delight, its pain!   What I mourn, know I not,

Unglückliche Liebe

Unhappy love   Wolfgang Amadeus Mozart (1756–91) KV520

Background

Gabriele von Baumberg moved in the same Viennese literary circles as Mozart. Mozart found the text to this song (written in 1787) in the *Wiener Musenalmanach* (Vienna Muses Almanac, 1786); von Baumberg's collection *Sämmtliche Gedichte* (Complete Poems) was not published until 1800. Mozart composed this song for his friend Gottfried von Jacquin to use in courtship and even allowed him to publish it under his own name in 1791. Unusually perhaps, compared to his more lyrical songs, Mozart here treats the poem almost as a recitative, displaying a closer engagement with the text than normally found in Viennese Lieder of the period. This song is also known as 'Als Luise die Briefe ihres ungetreuen Liebhabers verbrannte' (When Louise burnt her unfaithful lover's letters).

Idiomatic translation

Produced by fervent fantasy,
In a rapturous moment!
Perish, you children of melancholy!

You owe your existence to the flames,
I now give you back to flames again,
And all those rapturous songs;
For ah! he did not sing for me alone.

You are burning now, and soon, my dears,
There will be no further trace of you left:
But ah! the man who wrote you
May yet burn long in my heart.

Pronunciation – Unglückliche Liebe [ʊnɡlʏklɪçə liːbə]

Erzeugt von heißer Phantasie,
ɛɐtsoikt fɔn haisɐ fantaziː

in einer schwärmerischen Stunde
|ɪn |ainə ʃvɛrmərɪʃən   ʃtʊndə

zur Welt gebrachte! – geht zu Grunde!
tsuːɐ vɛlt ɡəbraxtə   ɡeːt tsuː ɡrʊndə

Ihr Kinder der Melancholie!
|iːɐ kɪndɐ deːɐ melankoliː

Ihr danket Flammen euer Sein:
|iːɐ dankət flamən |oiɐ zain

ich geb' euch nun den Flammen wieder,
|ɪç ɡeːp |oiç nuːn deːn flamən   viːdɐ

und all die schwärmerischen Lieder;
|ʊnt |al diː ʃvɛrmərɪʃən   liːdɐ

denn ach! er sang nicht mir allein.
dɛn |ax |eːɐ zaŋ nɪçt miːɐ |alain

Ihr brennet nun, und bald, ihr Lieben,
|iːɐ brɛnət nuːn |ʊnt balt |iːɐ liːbən

ist keine Spur von euch mehr hier:
|ɪst kainə ʃpuːɐ fɔn |oiç meːɐ hiːɐ

Doch ach! der Mann, der euch geschrieben,
dɔx |ax deːɐ man deːɐ |oiç ɡəʃriːbən

brennt lange noch vielleicht in mir.
brɛnt laŋə nɔx fiːlaiçt |ɪn miːɐ

Further notes

In the word **Melancholie**, note that the pronunciation of the first syllable has a closed [e] but without the usual lengthening [eː]. This is due to the foreign origin of the word.

Unglückliche Liebe

Unhappy love

CD1  *spoken text*
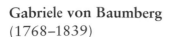 *piano accompaniment*

Gabriele von Baumberg
(1768–1839)

W.A. Mozart KV 520
(1756–91)

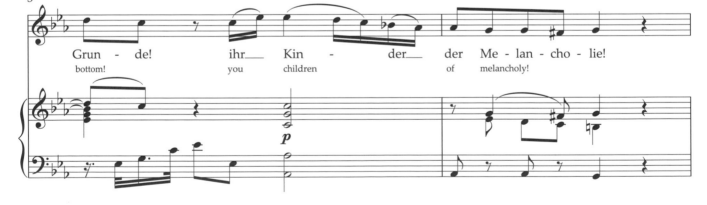

Sein: ich geb' euch nun den Flam - men
being: I give you now to-the flames

wie - der, und all die schwär - me - ri - - schen
again, and all the rapturous

Lie - der; denn ach! er sang nicht mir al -
songs for ah! he sang not to-me alone.

- lein. Ihr bren - net nun, und bald, ihr
You burn - net now, and soon you

Du bist wie eine Blume

You are like a flower   Robert Schumann (1810–56) Op. 25 No. 24

Background

Like 'Widmung', which appears earlier in this volume, 'Du bist wie eine Blume' comes from the cycle *Myrthen, Liederkries* ('Myrtles, Song-cycle'), which consists of twenty-six songs composed by Schumann in February 1840 as a wedding present for his beloved Clara Wieck. Of all Heine's poems, its direct simplicity and intimacy has led to it being set by more composers than any other. As with 'Widmung' and others in this cycle, 'Clara themes' are hidden in the accompaniment and elsewhere, and this song was apparently a particular favourite of Clara's.

Idiomatic translation

You are like a flower,
so dear and beautiful and pure;
I look at you and melancholy
steals into my heart.

I feel as if I should lay
my hands upon your head,
praying that God preserves you
so pure and beautiful and dear.

Pronunciation – Du bist wie eine Blume [du: bɪst vi: |ainə blu:mə]

Du bist wie eine Blume,
du: bist vi: |ainə blu:mə

so hold und schön und rein;
zo: hɔlt |ʊnt ʃøːn |ʊnt rain

ich schau' dich an, und Wehmut
|ɪç ʃau dɪç |an |ʊnt veːmuːt

schleicht mir in's Herz hinein.
ʃlaiçt miːɐ |ɪns hɛrts hɪnain

Mir ist, als ob ich die Hände
miːɐ |ɪst |als |ɔp |ɪç di: hɛndə

auf's Haupt dir legen sollt',
|aufs haupt diːɐ leːgən zɔlt

betend, daß Gott dich erhalte
beːtənt das gɔt dɪç |ɛɐhaltə

so rein und schön und hold.
zo: rain |ʊnt ʃøːn |ʊnt hɔlt

CD1 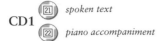 spoken text
piano accompaniment

Du bist wie eine Blume

You are like a flower

Heinrich Heine
(1797–1856)

Robert Schumann Op. 25 No. 24
(1810–56)

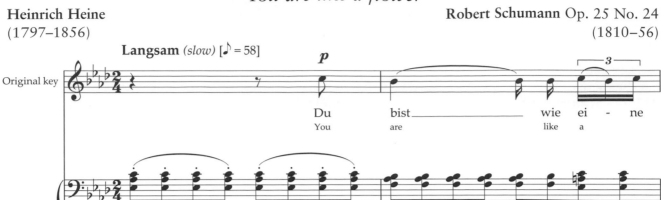

Blu- me, so hold und schön und rein;
flower, so dear and beautiful and pure;

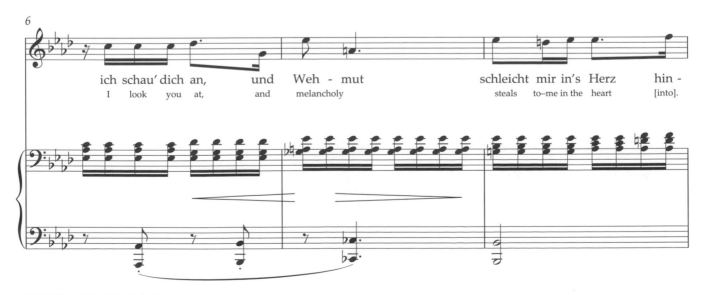

ich schau' dich an, und Weh-mut
I look you at, and melancholy

schleicht mir in's Herz hin-
steals to-me in the heart [into].

Wir wandelten

We wandered   Johannes Brahms (1833–97) Op. 96 No. 2

Background

Georg Daumer's poetry was frequently set by Brahms, and amidst more humanist themes of physical and spiritual unity there is an underlying eroticism infusing many of the lyrics. This poem, written around 1884, comes from Daumer's *Polydora, ein weltpoetisches Liederbuch* (Polydora, a world-poetic song book) of 1855. It is a translation from the Magyar, and the fusion of text and music is especially notable here. The bells referred to in the poem appear in the opening bars of the piano prelude and symbolise eternal unity between the lovers – their two melodies are interwoven in various ways throughout the song.

Idiomatic translation

We wandered, we two together,
I was so silent and you so silent,
I would give much to learn
What you were thinking at that moment.

What I was thinking, let it remain unspoken!
Only one thing shall I say:
So beautiful was all that I thought,
So heavenly and serene was it all.

The thoughts in my head
Rang like little golden bells;
So wondrously sweet and lovely
is no other sound in the world.

Pronunciation – **Wir wandelten** [viːɐ vandɛltən]

Wir wandelten, wir zwei zusammen,
viːɐ vandɛltən viːɐ tsvai tsuːzamən

ich war so still und du so stille;
|ɪç vaːr zoː ʃtɪl |ʊnt duː zoː ʃtɪlə

ich gäbe viel, um zu erfahren,
|ɪç geːbə fiːl |ʊm tsuː |ɛɐfaːrən

was du gedacht in jenem Fall.
vas duː gədaxt |ɪn jeːnəm fal

Was ich gedacht, unausgesprochen
vas |ɪç gədaxt |ʊn|ausgəʃprɔxən

verbleibe das! Nur Eines sag' ich:
fɛɐblaibə das nuːɐ |ainəs zak |ɪç

So schön war alles, was ich dachte,
zoː ʃøːn vaːr |aləs vas |ɪç daxtə

so himmlisch heiter war es all' …
zoː hɪmlɪʃ haitɐ vaːr |ɛs |al

In meinem Haupte die Gedanken,
|ɪn mainəm hauptə diː gədankən

sie läuteten wie gold'ne Glöckchen;
ziː loitətən viː gɔldnə glœkçən

so wundersüss, so wunderlieblich
zoː vʊndɐzyːs zoː vʊndɐliːplɪç

ist in der Welt kein and'rer Hall.
|ɪst |ɪn deːɐ vɛlt kain |andɐ hal

Further notes

Note that in some composite words in German – such as **unausgesprochen** – glottal stops occur in the middle of the word and need to be marked.

Wir wandelten
We wandered

CD1 [23] *spoken text*
[24] *piano accompaniment*

Georg Friedrich Daumer
(1800–75)

Johannes Brahms Op. 96 No. 2
(1833–97)

Original key

Andante espressivo [♩ = 70]

p dolce

dolce

Wir wan-del-ten, wir zwei zu-sam - men,
We wandered, we two together,

ich___ war so still und du so stil - le; ich gä - be
I was so silent and you so silent; I would–give

viel, um zu er-fah - ren, was du ge-dacht in je-nem Fall. Was
much in–order to to–learn, what you thought in that case. What

ich ge-dacht, un - aus-ge-spro - chen ver-blei-be das! Nur
I thought, unspoken remains that! Only

Ei - nes sag' ich, Ei - nes sag' ich: So schön war al - les,
one–thing say I, one–thing say I: so beautiful was all,

was ich dach-te, so himm-lisch hei - ter war es all'...
which I thought, so heavenly serene was it all...

In mei-nem Haup-te die Ge - dan-ken, sie läu-te-
In my head the thoughts, they rang

Die Nacht

The night Richard Strauss (1864–1949) Op. 10 No. 3

Background

Richard Strauss was born into a professional musical family in Munich. He was to become a well-known conductor (though with a controversial reputation for working with the Nazi party) and composer, and is renowned for developing the symphonic tone poem (*Don Juan* 1889, *Till Eulenspiegels lustige Streiche* 1894–95, *Also sprach Zarathustra* 1896, *Don Quixote* 1897) and composing operas (*Salome* 1905, *Der Rosenkavalier* 1910, *Ariadne auf Naxos* 1912, *Capriccio* 1941). He married the famously free-spirited soprano Pauline de Ahna, and throughout his life preferred the soprano voice to all others; he wrote over two hundred lieder in his lifetime. This early song was written in 1885, using words by the controversial Austrian poet Hermann von Gilm, whose poems were widely denounced for being anti-Jesuit.

Idiomatic translation

Night steps out of the forest,
Creeps softly from the trees,
Looks around in a wide circle,
Now take care!

All the lights of this world,
All the flowers, all the colours
She extinguishes and steals the sheaves
From the field.

She takes everything that is dear,
Takes the silver from the river,
Takes from the cathedral's copper roof
The gold.

The bush stands plundered:
Move closer, soul to soul,
O the night, I fear, might steal
You from me too.

Pronunciation – Die Nacht [diː naxt]

Aus dem Walde tritt die Nacht,
|aus deːm valdə trɪt diː naxt

aus den Bäumen schleicht sie leise,
|aus deːn bɔimən ʃlaiçt zi: laizə

schaut sich um in weitem Kreise,
ʃaut ziç |ʊm |ɪn vaitəm kraizə

nun gib Acht!
nuːn gɪp |axt

Alle Lichter dieser Welt,
|alə lɪçtɐ diːzɐ vɛlt

alle Blumen, alle Farben
|alə bluːmən |alə farbən

löscht sie aus und stiehlt die Garben
løʃt zi: |aus |ʊnt ʃtiːlt di: garbən

weg vom Feld.
vɛk fɔm fɛlt

Alles nimmt sie, was nur hold,
|aləs nɪmt zi: vas nuːɐ hɔlt

nimmt das Silber weg des Stroms,
nɪmt das zɪlbɐ vɛk des ʃtroːms

nimmt vom Kupferdach des Doms
nɪmt fɔm kʊpfɐdax des doːms

weg das Gold.
vɛk das gɔlt

Ausgeplündert steht der Strauch,
|ausgəplʏndɐt ʃteːt deːɐ straux

rükke näher, Seel' an Seele;
rʏkə neːɐ zeːl |an zeːlə

o die Nacht, mir bangt, sie stehle
|oː di: naxt miːɐ baŋt zi: ʃteːlə

dich mir auch.
dɪç miːɐ |aux

Further notes

Note that the pronunciation of the verb **weg** is [vɛk]. Do not confuse it with the noun **der Weg** [veːk]. The *r* in **Ausgeplündert** is not pronounced, in order to preserve the musical line at this moment. This is, however, open to individual artistic interpretation.

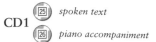

Die Nacht
The night

Hermann von Gilm
(1812–64)

Richard Strauss Op. 10 No. 3
(1864–1949)

Après un rêve

After a dream

Gabriel Fauré (1845–1924) Op. 7 No. 1

Background

Fauré's musical gifts were recognised as a child when an elderly blind woman heard him playing the harmonium in a local chapel. He was sent to study in Paris at L'École Niedermeyer, where he met Saint-Saëns. Although he was to earn his living primarily as an organist, by the time he was twenty he had published twenty songs. This is a setting of a poem by Romain Bussine (1830–99), professor of singing at the Paris Conservatoire, and was taken from an anonymous Tuscan text entitled 'Levati sol che la luna é levatai'. The song was composed in 1877–78, around the time that his hopes of marriage to Pauline Viardot's daughter Marianne were dashed – hence the song's subject matter. Its famous melody has also inspired several instrumental arrangements, most notably a setting for cello and piano by Pablo Casals.

Idiomatic translation

In a slumber, charmed by your image,
I dreamed of happiness, burning mirage.
Your eyes were more soft, your voice pure and ringing;
You shone like a sky lit up by daybreak;
You were calling me, and I left the earth
To flee with you towards the light.

The heavens parted their clouds for us,
Splendours unknown, glimpses of divine light.
Alas! Alas, sad awakening from dreams!
I call to you, o night, give me back your illusions;
Return, return radiant,
Return, o mysterious night!

Pronunciation – **Après un rêve** [apʀɛ(z)œ̃ ʀɛv]

Dans un sommeil que charmait ton image
dɑ̃(z)œ̃ sɔmɛj kə ʃaʀmɛ tõ(n)imaʒə

Je rêvais le bonheur, ardent mirage,
ʒə ʀɛve lə bɔnœʀ aʀdɑ̃ miʀaʒə

Tes yeux étaient plus doux, ta voix pure et sonore,
tɛ(z)jø(z)ete ply du ta vwa py(ʀ)e sɔnɔʀə

Tu rayonnais comme un ciel éclairé par l'aurore;
ty ʀɛjɔne kɔ(m)œ̃ sjɛ(l)eklɛʀe paʀ lɔʀɔʀə

Tu m'appelais | et je quittais la terre
ty mapəlɛ e ʒə kite la tɛʀə

Pour m'enfuir avec toi vers la lumière.
puʀ mɑ̃fɥi(ʀ)avɛk twa vɛʀ la lymjɛʀə

Les cieux pour nous | entr'ouvraient leurs nues,
le sjø puʀ nu ɑ̃tʀuvʀɛ lœʀ nyə

Splendeurs inconnues, lueurs divines entrevues.
splɑ̃dœʀ(z)ɛ̃cɔnyə lyœʀ divinə(z)ɑ̃tʀəvyə

Hélas! hélas, triste réveil des songes,
elas elas tʀistə revɛj dɛ sõʒə

Je t'appelle, ô nuit, rends-moi tes mensonges;
ʒə tapɛlə o nɥi ʀɑ̃ mwa tɛ mɑ̃sõʒə

Reviens, reviens, radieuse,
ʀəvjɛ̃ ʀəvjɛ̃ ʀadiøzə

Reviens, ô nuit mystérieuse!
ʀəvjɛ̃ o nɥi misteʀiøzə

Further notes

Note the vocalic harmonisation within the word **éclairé** (see the key to French pronunciation at the back of this volume for an explanation of vocalic harmonisation). Note also that, in modern speech, the first syllable of **aurora** is pronounced with a more open [ɔ] sound. In singing however, a more 'elegant' rendition closes the syllable to [o], thus [oʀɔʀə].

CD2

1 *spoken text*
2 *piano accompaniment*

Après un rêve

After a dream

Romain Bussine
(1830–99)

Gabriel Fauré Op. 7 No. 1
(1845–1924)

Original key
C minor

Dans un som-meil que char-mait ton i - ma - ge
In a slumber that charmed your image

Je rê-vais le bon-heur, ar-dent mi-ra - - ge,
I dreamed (of) the happiness, ardent mirage,

Tes yeux é-taient plus doux, ta voix pure et so-no - re, Tu ray-on-
your eyes were more soft, your voice pure and resonant, you shone

-nais comme un ciel é-clai-ré par l'au-ro - re;
like a sky lit-up by the dawn;

Notre amour

Our love　　　　　　　　　　　　　　　　　　　Gabriel Fauré (1845–1924) Op. 23 No. 2

Background

Armand Silvestre was one of the Symbolist poets, whose works, like those of Paul Verlaine and Jean Lahor, moved away from traditional forms of poetry to embrace principles of freer versification, more fluidity and less precise description. Often criticised as rather sentimental, without much substance, Silvestre's poetry was nevertheless frequently set by composers such as Fauré, Duparc and Massenet. This song was composed around 1879. Fauré's songs were often first performed in the private homes of rich patrons in Paris by keen amateur singers, and many songs are dedicated to them (the alternative high note at the end of this song was probably inserted to accommodate a particular singer). Fauré believed that the voice should be a *porte-verbe* (carrier of words) and therefore preferred keys for medium voice as clarity of text is often lost in a high tessitura.

Idiomatic translation

Our love is something light,
like the perfumes that the wind
brings from the tips of ferns
for us to breathe in while dreaming.
Our love is something light!

Our love is something enchanting,
like the songs of the morning
where there are no expressions of regret,
where quivers uncertain hope.
Our love is something enchanting!

Our love is something sacred,
like the mysteries of the woods
where an unknown soul shivers,
where silences have voices.
Our love is something sacred!

Our love is something infinite,
like sunset paths,
where the ocean, reunited with the skies,
falls asleep beneath slanting suns.

Our love is something eternal,
like all that has been touched
by the fiery wing of a victorious god,
like all that comes from the heart.
Our love is something eternal!

Pronunciation – **Notre amour** [nɔtʀamuʀ]

Notre‿amour‿est chose légère,
nɔtʀamuʀɛ　　　ʃozə　leʒɛʀə

Comme les parfums que le vent
kɔmə　　lɛ　paʀfœ̃　kə　lə　vã

Prend‿aux cimes de la fougère
pʀã(t)o　　simə　də la fuʒɛʀə

Pour qu'on les respire‿en rêvant.
puʀ kõ　　lɛ　ʀɛspiʀã　ʀevã

Notre amour‿est chose légère!
nɔtʀamuʀɛ　　　ʃozə　leʒɛʀə

Notre‿amour‿est chose charmante,
nɔtʀamuʀɛ　　　ʃozə　ʃaʀmãtə

Comme les chansons du matin
kɔmə　　lɛ　ʃãsõ　　dy matɛ̃

Où nul regret ne se lamente,
u　　nyl ʀəgʀɛ　nə sə lamãtə

Où vibre‿un‿espoir‿incertain.
u　　vib(ʀ)œ̃(n)ɛspwaʀɛ̃sɛʀtɛ̃

Notre‿amour‿est chose charmante!
nɔtʀamuʀɛ　　　ʃozə　ʃaʀmãtə

Notre‿amour est chose sacrée,
nɔtʀamuʀɛ　　　ʃozə　sakʀeə

Comme les mystères des bois
kɔmə　　lɛ　mistɛʀə　dɛ bwa

Où tressaille‿une‿âme‿ignorée,
u　　tʀesajy(n)a(m)iɲɔʀeə

Où les silences‿ont des voix.
u　　lɛ　silãsə(z)õ　dɛ vwa

Notre‿amour‿est chose sacrée!
nɔtʀamuʀɛ　　　ʃozə　sakʀeə

Notre‿amour‿est chose‿infinie,
nɔtʀamuʀɛ　　　ʃo(z)ɛ̃finiə

Comme les chemins des couchants
kɔmə　　lɛ　ʃəmɛ̃　　dɛ kuʃã

Où la mer,‿aux cieux réunie,
u　　la mɛʀo　　sjø　　reyniə

S'endort sous les soleils penchants.
sãdɔʀ　sus lɛ　sɔlɛj　pãʃã

Notre‿amour‿est chose‿éternelle,
nɔtʀamuʀɛ ʃo(z)etɛʀnɛlə

Comme tout ce qu'un dieu vainqueur
kɔmə tu sə kœ̃ djø vɛ̃kœʀ

A touché du feu de son‿aile,
a tuʃe dy fø də sõ(n)ɛlə

Comme tout ce qui vient du coeur,
kɔmə tu sə ki vjɛ̃ dy kœʀ

Notre‿amour‿est chose‿éternelle!
nɔtʀamuʀɛ ʃo(z)etɛʀnɛlə

Further notes

Several lines of text have many liaisons. Check the phonetics carefully for accuracy.

CD2   spoken text
  piano accompaniment

Notre amour
Our love

Armand Silvestre
(1837–1901)

Gabriel Fauré Op. 23 No. 2
(1845–1924)

Original key

p leggieramente

p leggiero e legato

Notre a - mour est cho - se lé - gè - re,   Com - me les par - fums que le vent   Prend aux
Our love is (a) thing light,   like the perfumes that the wind takes from—the

ci - mes de la fou - gè - re   Pour qu'on les res - pire en rê - vant.   Notre a -
tips of the ferns   in—order that one them breathes while dreaming.   Our love

-mour est cho - se lé - gè - re!
is (a) thing light!

Les roses d'Ispahan

The roses of Isfahan   Gabriel Fauré (1845–1924) Op. 39 No. 4

Background

This setting of a poem by Leconte de Lisle (1818–94) was composed in 1884, and forms part of the second collection of Fauré's songs published by Hamelle. De Lisle was the leading light amongst a group of poets known as the Parnassians, who emphasised clarity and form in their works, often choosing exotic or classical subjects, rich in colourful imagery, which were then treated with a certain objectivity and detachment. Here, the rocking movement of the piano accompaniment evokes the swaying journey of the traveller, and the harmonies conjure up the sultry heat of Persia.

Idiomatic translation

The roses of Isfahan in their sheath of moss,
the jasmines of Mosul, the orange blossoms,
have a perfume less fresh, a fragrance less sweet,
o pale Leila, than your soft breath!

Your lips are coral and your light laughter
sounds better than running water, and has a voice more sweet.
Better than the joyous breeze that rocks the orange-tree,
better than the bird that sings on the edge of its nest of moss.

O Leila, ever since in their airy flight
all the kisses have fled from your lips so sweet,
there is no longer any fragrance from the pale orange-tree,
no heavenly aroma from the roses in the moss.

Oh, that your youthful love, that light butterfly,
would return to my heart on swift and sweet wings
and perfume once more the orange blossom
and the roses of Isfahan in their sheath of moss.

Pronunciation – Les roses d'Ispahan [lɛ ʀoz dispaã]

Les roses d'Ispahan dans leur gaîne de mousse,
lɛ ʀozə dispaã   dã   lœʀ gɛnə də musə

Les jasmins de Mossoul, les fleurs de l'oranger,
lɛ ʒasmɛ̃ də mosul   lɛ flœʀ də lɔʀãʒe

Ont un parfum moins frais, | ont une odeur moins douce,
õ(t)œ̃ paʀfœ̃ mwɛ̃ fʀɛ   õ(t)ynɔdœʀ   mwɛ̃ dusə

Ô blanche Leïlah! que ton souffle léger.
o blãʃə   Leila kə tõ suflə leʒe

Ta lèvre est de corail et ton rire léger
ta lɛvʀɛ   də kɔʀaj e tõ ʀiʀə leʒe

Sonne mieux que l'eau vive et d'une voix plus douce,
sɔnə mjø kə lo vive dynə vwa ply dusə

Mieux que le vent joyeux qui berce l'oranger,
mjø   kə lə vã ʒwajø ki bɛʀsə lɔʀãʒe

Mieux que l'oiseau qui chante au bord d'un nid de mousse.
mjø kə lwazo ki ʃãto   bɔʀ dœ̃ ni də musə

Ô Leïlah! depuis que de leur vol léger
o leila   dəpɥi kə də lœʀ vɔl leʒe

Tous les baisers | ont fui de ta lèvre si douce,
tu   lɛ beze   õ fɥi də ta lɛvʀə si dusə

Il n'est plus de parfum dans le pâle oranger,
il nɛ ply də paʀfœ̃ dã le palɔʀãʒe

Ni de céleste arôme aux roses dans leur mousse.
ni də selɛstaʀomo   ʀozə dã   lœʀ musə

Oh! que ton jeune amour, ce papillon léger,
o   kə tõ ʒœnamur   sə papijõ leʒe

Revienne vers mon cœur d'une aile prompte et douce,
ʀəvjɛnə vɛʀ mõ kœʀ dynɛlə   pʀõte   dusə

Et qu'il parfume encor la fleur de l'oranger,
e kil paʀfymãkɔʀ   la flœʀ də lɔʀãʒe

Les roses d'Ispahan dans leur gaine de mousse.
lɛ ʀozə dispaã   dã   lœʀ gɛnə də musə

Further notes

In the word **prompte** the second *p* is silent.

Les roses d'Ispahan
The roses of Isfahan

Charles-Marie-René Leconte de Lisle
(1818–94)

Gabriel Fauré Op. 39 No. 4
(1845–1924)

CD2
5 *spoken text*
6 *piano accompaniment*

Original key
D major

Les ro - ses d'Is-pa-han dans leur gaî-ne de mous - se, Les jas-
The roses of Isfahan in their covering of moss, the

-mins de Mos-soul, les fleurs de l'o-ran - ger,
jasmines of Mosul, the flowers of the orange–tree,

Ont un par-fum moins frais, ont u-ne o-deur moins dou - ce, Ô blan - che
have a perfume less fresh, have a fragrance less sweet, o white

Les filles de Cadix

The girls of Cadiz   Pauline Viardot (1821–1910)

Background

Born into the illustrious and musical García family, and sister of the singer and composer Maria Malibran, Pauline Viardot was one of the most influential musical figures of her generation. She moved in glittering musical and intellectual circles and formed a lifelong friendship with Clara Schumann; she also played duets with Chopin. A celebrated mezzo-soprano, Pauline performed all the major operas of the day. Meyerbeer wrote a starring role for her in *Le prophète* and Berlioz engaged her to sing 'Orphée' in his French revival of Gluck's *Orfeo ed Euridice*. Brahms (a great lover of the mezzo voice) wrote his *Alto Rhapsody* for her. After a while, such varied repertoire began to affect her voice and Viardot turned to teaching, at which she excelled. She also began composing, and there are some 100 songs to her name, written for her pupils and the developing voice. She was quoted as saying, "Don't do what I did … I wanted to sing all things and I spoilt my voice." This poem was written by Alfred de Musset, who first met Pauline at her inaugural recital in Paris. It forms the final song in the set *Six mélodies* published in 1888. Cadiz is a port on Spain's south coast. The girls enjoy youthful fun at bullfights and dances and are not impressed by the conceited finery of a young nobleman who tries to attract them with his gold.

Idiomatic translation

We had just come from the bullfight,
Three boys, three girls.
On the grass the weather was fair,
And we were dancing a bolero
To the sound of castanets;
"Tell me, neighbour,
If I am looking nice,
And if my skirt
Suits me, this morning.
Do you think my waist slender?
Ah! Ah!
The girls of Cadiz rather like that."

And we were dancing a bolero
One Sunday evening,
A hidalgo* came towards us,
Covered in gold, a feather in his hat,
And his hand on his hip:
"If you fancy me,
Brunette with the sweet smile,
You have only to say so, and
This gold is yours."
"Go on your way, fine sir,
Ah! Ah!
The girls of Cadiz don't listen to that."

Pronunciation – Les filles de Cadix [lɛ fij də kadiks]

Nous venions de voir le taureau,
nu vənjõ də vwaʀ lə tɔʀo

Trois garçons, trois fillettes,
tʀwa gaʀsõ tʀwa fijetə

Sur la pelouse il faisait beau
syʀ la pəlu(z)il fəzɛ bo

Et nous dansions un boléro
e nu dãsjõ(z)œ̃ bɔleʀo

Au son des castagnettes.
o sõ dɛ kastaɲetə

"Dites-moi, voisin,
ditə mwa vwazɛ̃

Si j'ai bonne mine,
si ʒe bɔnə minə

Et si ma basquine
e si ma baskinə

Va bien, ce matin.
va bjɛ̃ sə matɛ̃

Vous me trouvez la taille fine?
vu mə tʀuve la tajə finə

Ah, ah!
ɑ ɑ

Les filles de Cadix aiment assez cela."
lɛ fijə də kadiksɛmə(t)ase səla

Et nous dansions un boléro,
e nu dãsjõ(z)œ̃ bɔleʀo

Un soir c'était dimanche.
œ̃ swaʀ setɛ dimãʃə

Vers nous s'en vint un hidalgo,
vɛʀ nu sã vɛ̃(t)œ̃(n)idalgo

Tout cousu d'or, plume au chapeau,
tu kuzy dɔʀ ply(m)o ʃapo

Et le poing sur la hanche:
e lə pwɛ̃ syʀ la |ãʃə

"Si tu veux de moi,
si ty vø də mwa

Brune au doux sourire,
bʀyno du suʀiʀə

Tu n'as qu'à le dire,
ty na ka lə diʀə

Cet or est à toi."
sɛ(t)ɔ(ʀ)ɛ(t)a twa

"Passez votre chemin, beau sire.
pase vɔtʀə ʃəmɛ̃ bo siʀə

Ah, ah!
ɑ ɑ

Les filles de Cadix n'entendent pas cela."
lɛ fijə də kadiks nãtãdə pɑ səla

Further notes

* Hidalgo = a gentleman of lower Spanish nobility.

CD2

7 spoken text
8 piano accompaniment

Les filles de Cadix

The girls of Cadiz

Alfred de Musset
(1810–57)

Pauline Viardot
(1821–1910)

© 2008 by Faber Music Ltd

* Recording cue

Villanelle

Villanelle   Hector Berlioz (1803–69) Op. 7 No. 1

from *Les nuits d'été*

Background

Hector Berlioz was born in Lyon. He was destined to study medicine, but instead turned to a career in music and composition, even though he was formally untrained. Berlioz struggled to find recognition as a composer in France during his lifetime, but became a successful conductor. Nevertheless, he had a lasting legacy as a composer: he influenced the development of the symphonic form and orchestral instrumentation in the 19th century. His best known works are *Symphonie fantastique* (1830), the operas *Les troyens* (1858) and *La damnation de Faust* (1845), and the oratorio *Grand messe des morts* (*Requiem* 1837). He also wrote over fifty songs (the term 'mélodie' was first used by Berlioz when referring to song) and 'Villanelle' is the first in a cycle of six songs entitled *Les nuits d'été* ('Summer nights', 1840–41) by the poet Théophile Gautier, which Berlioz later orchestrated.

Idiomatic translation

When the new season comes,
When the cold has disappeared,
We shall go together, my darling,
To gather the lily-of-the-valley in the wood.
Our tread scattering the pearls of dew
That are seen trembling in the morning,
We shall go to hear the blackbirds
Warbling.

The spring has come, my darling,
It is the month blessed by lovers;
And the bird, glossing its wing,
Sings verses on the edge of its nest.
Oh! Come then to this mossy bank,
To speak of our beautiful love,
And tell me with your gentle voice:
Always!

Far, far away, straying from our paths,
Let us startle the rabbit from his hiding-place,
And the deer, in the mirror of the springs
Admiring his lowered antlers;
Then back home, totally happy and at ease,
Our fingers interlaced for baskets,
Let us return, bringing back wild
Strawberries.

Pronunciation – **Villanelle** [vilanɛl]

Quand viendra la saison nouvelle,
kɑ̃   vjɛ̃dʀa la sɛzõ   nuvelə

Quand auront disparu les froids,
kɑ̃(t)oʀõ   dispaʀy le fʀwa

Tous les deux nous irons, ma belle,
tu   le dø   nu(z)iʀõ   ma bɛlə

Pour cueillir le muguet | aux bois.
puʀ kœjiʀ lə mygɛ   o   bwa

Sous nos pieds | égrenant les perles,
su   no pje   egʀənɑ̃ le pɛʀlə

Que l'on voit | au matin trembler,
kə   lõ   vwa o matɛ̃ tʀɑ̃ble

Nous irons écouter les merles siffler.
nu(z)iʀõ(z)ekute   le mɛʀlə sifle

Le printemps | est venu, ma belle,
lə   pʀɛ̃tɑ̃   ɛ   vəny ma bɛlə

C'est le mois des amants béni;
sɛ   lə mwa dɛ(z)amɑ̃   beni

Et l'oiseau, satinant son aile,
e   lwazo   satinɑ̃   sõ(n)ɛlə

Dit ses vers | au rebord du nid.
di sɛ vɛʀ o ʀəbɔʀ dy ni

Oh! Viens donc, sur ce banc de mousse,
o   vjɛ̃   dõ   syʀ sə bɑ̃   də musə

Pour parler de nos beaux amours,
puʀ paʀle də no bo(z)amuʀ

Et dis-moi de ta voix si douce: Toujours!
e   di mwa də ta vwa si dusə   tuʒuʀ

Loin, bien loin, | égarant nos courses,
lwɛ̃ bjɛ̃ lwɛ̃ egaʀɑ̃ no kuʀsə

Faisons fuir le lapin caché,
fəzõ fɥiʀ lə lapɛ̃ kaʃe,

Et le daim, | au miroir   des sources
e lə dɛ̃   o miʀwaʀ dɛ suʀsə

Admirant son grand bois penché;
admiʀɑ̃ sõ gʀɑ̃ bwa pɑ̃ʃe

Puis chez nous, tout‿heureux, tout‿aises,
pɥi ʃe nu tu(t)œʀø   tu(t)ɛzə

En paniers | enlaçant nos doigts,
ɑ̃ panje ɑ̃lasɑ̃   no dwa

Revenons, rapportant des fraises des bois.
ʀəvənõ   ʀapɔʀtɑ̃   dɛ fʀɛzə dɛ bwa

Further notes

As the word **donc** is mid-sentence (and not followed by a vowel), the final *c* is not pronounced. See also **banc**.

Villanelle

Villanelle

CD2 [9] spoken text [10] piano accompaniment

Théophile Gautier
(1811–72)

Hector Berlioz Op. 7 No. 1
(1803–69)

Chanson triste

Song of sorrow   Henri Duparc (1848–1933)

Background

Henri Duparc was born in Paris and studied piano under César Franck at the Jesuit College of Vaugirard. His great reputation as a composer of the French Mélodie rests on some sixteen surviving solo songs, which he wrote between the ages of 20 and 37. He lived until he was 85 but tragically, due to a mysterious nervous illness, wrote nothing for the rest of his life, and was so critical of what he had written that much was destroyed. Set to a text by the Symbolist poet Jean Lahor, 'Chanson triste' is the earliest of the songs written in 1868 and is dedicated to Leon MacSwiney, his future brother-in-law. It forms a youthful expression of the typical French poetic concept of 'ecstatic melancholy'. Duparc went on to orchestrate this song some years later.

Idiomatic translation

In your heart, there sleeps moonlight,
A soft summer moonlight,
And to escape the cares of life
I will drown myself in your light.

I will forget past sorrows,
My love, when you cradle
My sad heart and my thoughts
In the loving calm of your arms.

You will take my poorly head,
Ah! sometimes on your lap,
And tell it a ballad
That will seem to speak of us;

And in your eyes full of sorrows,
In your eyes then I shall drink
So many kisses and so much tenderness
That perhaps I shall be healed.

Pronunciation – Chanson triste [ʃɑ̃sõ tʀist]

Dans ton cœur dor(t) un clair de lune,
dɑ̃   tõ   kœr dɔr   œ̃   klɛr də lynə

Un doux clair de lune d'été,
œ̃   du   klɛr də lynə dete

Et pour fuir la vie importune,
e   puʀ fɥiʀ la vi   ɛ̃pɔʀtynə

Je me noierai dans ta clarté.
ʒə mə nwaʀe dɑ̃   ta klaʀte

J'oublierai les douleurs passées,
ʒubliʀe   le dulœr   pase(ə)

Mon amour, quand tu berceras
mõ(n)amuʀ kɑ̃   ty bɛʀsəʀa

Mon triste cœur | et mes pensées
mõ   tʀistə kœr   e mɛ   pɑ̃se(ə)

Dans le calme aimant de tes bras.
dɑ̃   le kal(m)ɛmɑ̃   də tɛ bʀa

Tu prendras ma tête malade,
ty   pʀɑ̃dʀa   ma tɛtə maladə

Oh! quelquefois, sur tes genoux,
o   kɛlkəfwa   syʀ te ʒənu

Et lui diras | une ballade
e   lɥi diʀa ynə baladə

Qui semblera parler de nous;
ki   sɑ̃bləʀa paʀle də nu

Et dans tes yeux pleins de tristesse,
e dɑ̃ tɛ(z)jø plɛ̃   də tʀistɛsə

Dans tes yeux | alors je boirai
dɑ̃   tɛ(z)jø   alɔr ʒə bwaʀe

Tant de baisers | et de tendresses
tɑ̃   də beze   e də tɑ̃dʀɛsə

Que peut-être je guérirai.
kə   pøtɛtʀə ʒə geʀiʀe

Further notes

In speech, it would be normal to liaise **Et lui diras une ballade.** But in this case, because of the length of the note on **diras**, it is more elegant to leave out the liaison. In contemporary speech, the final mute *e* in **passées** and **pensées** can be avoided where the note remains the same. They are thus shown in brackets and not emphasised on the CD.

CD2 [11] spoken text
[12] piano accompaniment

Chanson triste
Song of sorrow

Jean Lahor
(1840–1909)

Henri Duparc
(1848–1933)

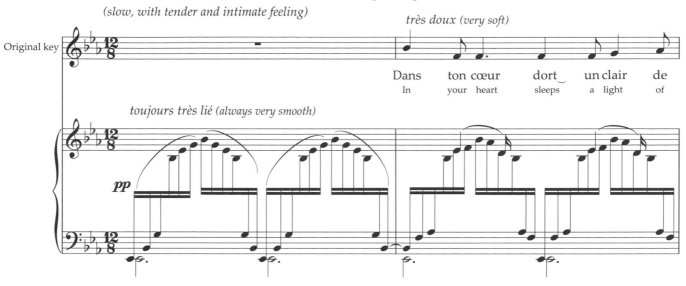

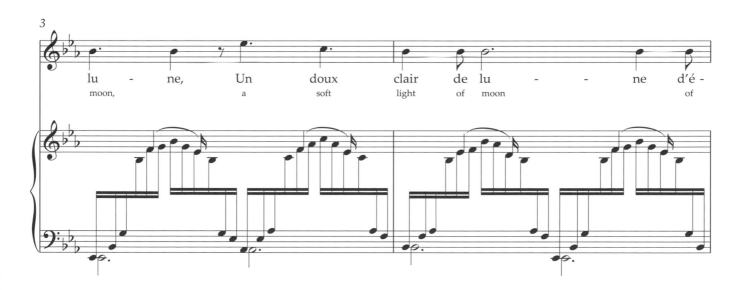

vie im-por-tu - ne, Je me noie - rai
life irksome, I (myself) will–drown

dans ta clar-té.
in your brightness.

J'ou - blie-rai les dou-leurs pas-
I will–forget the sorrows past,

-sé - es, Mon a-mour, quand tu ber-ce-ras Mon tris - te
my love, when you will–cradle my sad

Mandoline

Mandolin

Claude Debussy (1862–1918)

Background

Claude Debussy, born into a middle class family in St Germain-en-Laye, was one of the most influential composers of the 20th century. He was considered something of an outsider in the French musical tradition with his radical harmonies, and yet his music helped to define the musical aesthetic of the *fin-de-siècle* period. He composed in several genres, becoming the towering figure in the field of French song, but also wrote piano music (*Pour le piano*, *L'isle joyeuse*), orchestral pieces (*Ibéria*, *La mer*) and opera (*Pelléas et Mélisande*). Debussy began life as a promising pianist under the tutelage of Verlaine's mother-in-law, and to earn a living he played for singing lessons at the classes of Mme Moreau-Sainti where he was to develop a fascination for the singing voice. It was here that he met the older coloratura soprano Marie-Blanche Vasnier, with whom he embarked on an affair. This early song, written around 1882, is set to a text by the Symbolist poet Paul Verlaine and dedicated to Vasnier. Debussy was the first composer to set Verlaine's poetry, and many others were to follow suit, including Fauré who set this text in 1891.

Idiomatic translation

The serenaders
and the lovely listeners
exchange bland remarks
beneath the singing boughs.

There's Thyrsis and Amyntas,
and there's the tedious Clytander,
and there's Damis who, for many a
cruel woman, writes many a tender verse.

Their short silk jackets,
their long dresses with trains,
their elegance, their joy
and their soft blue shadows

Whirl in the ecstasy
of a pink and grey moon,
and the mandolin chatters
amidst the shivering breeze.

Pronunciation – Mandoline [mãdɔlin]

Les donneurs de sérénades
lɛ dɔnœʀ də seʀenadə

Leurs courtes vestes de soie,
lœʀ kuʀtə vɛstə də swa,

Et les belles écouteuses
e lɛ bɛlə(z)ekutøzə

Leurs longues robes à queues,
lœʀ lõgə ʀɔbə(z)a kø

Échangent des propos fades
eʃɑ̃ ʒə de pʀɔpo fadə

Leur élégance, leur joie
lœʀ elegɑ̃sə lœʀ jwa

Sous les ramures chanteuses.
su lɛ ʀamyʀə ʃɑ̃tøzə

Et leurs molles ombres bleues,
e lœʀ mɔlə(z)õbʀə blø

C'est Tircis et c'est Aminte,
sɛ tiʀsis e sɛ(t)amɛ̃tə

Tourbillonent dans l'extase
tuʀbijɔnə dɑ̃ lɛkstazə

Et c'est l'éternel Clitandre,
e sɛ letɛʀnɛl klitɑ̃dʀə

D'une lune rose et grise,
dynə lynə ʀo(z)e gʀizə

Et c'est Damis qui pour mainte
e sɛ damis ki puʀ mɛ̃tə

Et la mandoline jase
e la mãdɔlinə ʒazə

Cruelle fait maint vers tendre.
kʀyɛlə fɛ mɛ̃ vɛʀ tɑ̃dʀə

Parmi les frissons de brise.
paʀmi lɛ fʀisõ də bʀizə.

Further notes

Take care with the pronunciation of the names in this poem. Several final consonants are pronounced.

Mandoline

Mandolin

Paul Verlaine
(1844–96)

Claude Debussy
(1862–1918)

Les don-neurs de sé - ré-na-des
The givers of serenades

Et les bel - les é - cou-teu - ses
and the beautiful (female) listeners

É-chan - gent des pro-pos fa - des
exchange some remarks bland

Sous les ra - mu - res chan-teu - - - - ses.
under the boughs singing.

Le colibri

The humming-bird   **Ernest Chausson** (1855–99) Op. 2 No. 7

Background

Ernest Chausson went to the Paris Conservatoire to study composition under Jules Massenet at the unusually late age of twenty-five, having previously studied law. He stayed at the Conservatoire only a short time, however, before leaving to study privately with César Franck. Tragically killed in a bicycle accident in his mid-forties, Chausson wrote thirty-four songs in his brief life. 'Le colibri' was written around 1882, and is dedicated to Lady Harbord. It is a setting of the Parnassian poet Leconte de Lisle, who loved the exotic-sounding names of the flora and fauna depicted. The 5/4 time signature evokes something mysterious and other-wordly, while the vocal line radiates an ecstatic melancholy.

Idiomatic translation

The green humming-bird, the king of the hills,
Seeing the dew and the bright sun
Shining into his nest of fine woven grass,
Darts up into the air like a clear ray of light.

Hurriedly he flies to the nearby springs
Where the bamboos make a sound like the sea,
Where the red hibiscus with its heavenly scents
Opens and brings a humid light to the heart.

He descends towards the golden flower, alights,
And drinks so much love from the rosy cup
That he dies, not knowing if he could have drunk it dry.

On your pure lips, o my beloved,
Likewise, my soul would have wished to die
Of the first kiss which perfumed it.

Pronunciation – Le colibri [lə kɔlibʀi]

Le vert colibri, le roi des collines,
lə vɛʀ kɔlibʀi lə ʀwa de kɔlinə

Voyant la rosée et le soleil clair
vwajã la ʀoze e lə sɔlɛj klɛʀ

Luire dans son nid tissé d'herbes fines,
lɥiʀə dã sõ ni tise dɛʀbə finə

Comme un frais rayon s'échappe dans l'air.
kɔ(m)œ̃ fʀe ʀɛjõ seʃapə dã lɛʀ

Il se hâte | et vole aux sources voisines
il sə |ɑt e vɔ(l)o suʀsə vwazinə

Où les bambous font le bruit de la mer,
u lɛ bãbu fõ lə bʀɥi də la mɛʀ

Où l'açoka rouge aux odeurs divines,
u lasoka ʀu(ʒ)o(z)ɔdœʀ divinə

S'ouvre et porte au coeur un humide éclair.
suv(ʀ)e pɔʀ(t)o kœʀ œ̃(n)ymi(d)eklɛʀ

Vers la fleur dorée il descend, se pose,
vɛʀ la flœʀ dɔʀe il desã   sə pozə

Et boit tant d'amour dans la coupe rose,
e bwa tã damuʀ dã la kupə ʀozə

Qu'il meurt, ne sachant s'il l'a pu tarir.
kil mœʀ nə saʃã   sil la py taʀiʀ

Sur ta lèvre pure, | ô ma bien-aimée,
syʀ ta lɛvʀə pyʀə o ma bjɛ̃nemeə

Telle aussi mon âme eut voulu mourir,
tɛ(l)osi mõ(n)a(m)y vuly muʀiʀ

Du premier baiser qui l'a parfumée!
dy pʀəmje beze ki la paʀfymeə

CD2 [15] *spoken text*
[16] *piano accompaniment*

Le colibri
The humming-bird

Leconte de Lisle
(1818–94)

Ernest Chausson Op. 2 No. 7
(1855–99)

Pas vite (*not fast*) [♩ = 64]

Original key

mf

doux (*soft*)

Le vert co-li-bri, le roi des col-li-nes, Voy-ant la ro-sée et le so-leil
The green humming-bird, the king of–the hills, seeing the dew and the sun

clair Lui-re dans son nid tis-sé d'her-bes fi-nes,—
bright shining in its nest woven of grasses fine,

Comme un frais ra-yon s'é-chap-pe dans l'air.— Il se hâte— et vole aux sour-ces voi-
like a clear ray escaping in the air. He hurries and flies to–the sources

106

* Recording cue

C

C

from *Deux poèmes de Louis Aragon*, No. 1

Francis Poulenc (1899–1963)

Background

Poulenc was born in Paris and went on to become one of the 20th century's foremost composers of French song. The First World War interrupted his studies and so he never studied composition formally, but his piano teacher introduced him to Erik Satie who, along with George Auric, Darius Milhaud, Arthur Honegger, Louis Durey and Germaine Tailleferre, were to form the group known as *Les Six*. Poulenc frequented the renowned bookshop *La maison des amis des livres* (The house of the friends of books) where he met many literary figures and artists, including Picasso. His long association with baritone Pierre Bernac led to many songs being written for baritone. This song is the first in a pair of Louis Aragon settings, written during the German occupation in 1942. Aragon – a Marxist and deeply troubled by the events in France – had these poems published secretly. 'C' evokes the panic of the French population in May 1940 as thousands crossed the river Loire to escape the advancing German army. Aragon had been at the village of Ponts-de-Cé, near Angers, where the river was full of abandoned weapons and upturned vehicles.

Idiomatic translation

I have crossed the bridges of Cé	An eternal fiancée
It is there that everything began	And like iced milk I drank
A song of times past	The long lay of false glories
Speaks of a wounded knight	The Loire carries my thoughts away
Of a rose upon the carriageway	Along with the overturned cars
And of a bodice unlaced	And the unprimed weapons
Of the castle of an insane duke	And the ill-dried tears
And of the swans in its moats	O my France, my forsaken one
Of the meadow where comes to dance	I have crossed the bridges of Cé.

Pronunciation – C [se]

J'ai traversé les ponts de Cé
ʒe tʀavɛʀse le põ də se

C'est là que tout a commencé
sɛ la kə tu(t)a kɔmãse

Une chanson des temps passés
unə ʃãsõ dɛ tã pase

Parle d'un chevalier blessé
paʀlə dœ̃ ʃəvalje blese

D'une rose sur la chaussée
dynə ʀozə syʀ la ʃose*

Et d'un corsage délacé
e dœ̃ kɔʀsaʒə delase

Du château d'un duc insensé
dy ʃato dœ̃ dy(k)ɛ̃sãse

Et des cygnes dans les fossés
e dɛ siɲə dã le fose

De la prairie où vient danser
de la pʀɛʀi u vjɛ̃ dãse

Une éternelle fiancée
y(n)etɛʀnelə fijãse

Et j'ai bu comme un lait glacé
e ʒe by kɔmœ̃ lɛ glase

Le long lai des gloires faussées
lə lõ le dɛ glwaʀə fose

La Loire emporte mes pensées
la lwa(ʀ)ãpɔʀtə mɛ pãse

Avec les voitures versées
avɛk lɛ vwatyʀə vɛʀse

Et les armes désarmorcées
e lɛ(z)aʀmə dezaʀmɔʀse

Et les larmes mal effacées
e lɛ laʀmə malefase

O ma France, ô ma délaissée
o ma fʀãsə | o ma delese

j'ai traversé les ponts de Cé
ʒe tʀavɛʀse le põ də se

Further notes

* The last word of each line ends in *cé*, hence the title. The final mute *e* [ə], traditionally pronounced in poetic French at the ends of words ending in [se] (eg: **chaussée**), should therefore be omitted in order to fulfil the rhyming intentions of the poet.

CD2 spoken text
piano accompaniment

C

C

Louis Aragon
(1897–1982)

Francis Poulenc
(1899–1963)

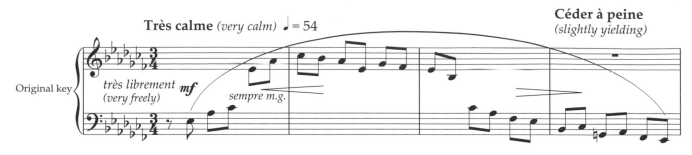

Céder un peu
(yield a little)

-teau d'un duc in - sen - sé___ Et des cy - gnes dans les fos - sés___ De
of a duke insane *and the swans in the moats* *of*

a tempo

infiniment doux (infinitely soft)

la prai - rie où vient dan - ser Une é - ter - nel - le fi - an - cé - e
the meadow where comes to–dance an eternal fiancée

doucement effleuré
(gently touched)

Et j'ai bu comme un lait gla - cé Le long lai des gloi - res faus - sé - es
and I have drunk like a milk iced the long lay of glories false

Нет, только тот, кто знал

None but the lonely heart　　　　　　　Pyotr Ilyich Tchaikovsky (1840–1893) Op. 6 No. 6

Background

Tchaikovsky, the son of a mining engineer and a mother of French ancestry, was born in the small town of Votkinsk. Being sent away to boarding school in St Petersburg at the age of ten, coupled with the sudden death of his beloved mother four years later, contributed to Tchaikovsky's sensitive and melancholic personality. Relationships with women were often idealised and it is widely believed that his struggles with homosexuality were to affect his life and music profoundly. In 1862 he began studying music under Zaremba at the St Petersburg Conservatory and went on to become a prolific composer, writing in many musical genres, including opera (*Queen of Spades* 1890 and *Eugene Onegin* 1878), orchestral music (six symphonies, *Romeo and Juliet* 1869–80, *1812 Overture* 1880), concertos for violin and piano, and ballet music (*Swan Lake* 1876 and *The Nutcracker* 1892). He also wrote over one hundred songs, and was commonly drawn to the theme of love and its loss. This popular song, written in 1869, uses the translation of Goethe's text *Nur wer die sehnsucht kennt* ('None but the lonely know'). It is one of the *Mignon* songs from *Wilhelm Meister* – the story of a young girl with a tragic past, rescued by Wilhelm from a travelling circus – and has come to represent the Romantic expression of the nostalgic search for a better and nobler world.

Idiomatic translation

Only one who has longed for a meeting (with a loved one)
can understand how I suffered and how I am still suffering.
I look into the distance ... I have no strength, my eyes grow dim ...
He who knew and loved me is far away!
Only one who has longed for a meeting (with a loved one)
can understand how I suffered and how I am still suffering.
My breast is burning ...
Only one who has longed for a meeting (with a loved one)
can understand how I suffered and how I am still suffering.

Pronunciation – Нет, только тот, кто знал [njɛt tɔljka tɔt ktɔ znɑl]

Нет, то́лько тот, кто знал
njɛt tɔljka　tɔt　ktɔ znɑl

свида́нья жа́жду,
svjidɑnja　ʒɑʒdu

поймёт, как я страда́л
paimjɔt　kak ja stradɑl

и как я стра́жду.
i　kak ja strɑʒdu

Гляжу́ я вдаль ... нет сил,
gljɪʒu　ja　vdalj....　njɛt sjil

тускне́ет око ...
tusknjɛjɪt　ɔkɑ

Ах, кто меня́ люби́л
ɑx　ktɔ　mjɪnja　ljubjil

и знал далёко!
i　znal　daljɔka

Вся грудь гори́т ...
fsja　grudj　garjit

Нет, только тот, кто знал
None but the lonely heart

Lev Aleksandrovich Mey
(1822–62)

Pyotr Ilyich Tchaikovsky Op. 6 No. 6
(1840–93)

Не верь, мой друг

Believe it not, my friend **Pyotr Ilyich Tchaikovsky (1840–93) Op. 6 No. 1**

Background

This song comes from Tchaikovsky's first set of six Romances written in 1869. Such songs would have been written for the private drawing-room and were settings of translations and of contemporary Russian writers, in this case Count Alexei Tolstoy, who was a distant relative of the great Russian writer Leo Tolstoy. Alexei Tolstoy worked at court in St Petersburg as Grand Master of Royal Hunting, and upon retiring from service devoted his time to writing poetry, novels and plays.

Idiomatic translation

Do not believe, my friend, when in an outburst of grief
I say I have ceased to love you!
At the hour of the ebb tide, do not believe that the sea is unfaithful,
It will lovingly come back to land.

I'm already yearning, full of the same old passion,
I will give my freedom to you again,
And already, the roaring waves are running back
From afar to the beloved shores.

Pronunciation – **Не верь, мой друг** [njɛ vjɛrj mɔi druk]

Не верь, мой друг, когда́ в поры́ве го́ря
njɛ vjɛrj mɔi druk kagda fparivjɛ gɔrja

Я говорю́, что разлюби́л тебя́,
ja gavarju ʃtɔ razljubjil tjɪbja

В отли́ва час не верь, изме́не мо́ря,
vatljiva tʃas njɛ vjɛrj izmjɛnjɛ mɔrja

Оно́ к земле́ воро́тится любя́.
anɔ kzjimljɛ varɔtjitsa ljubja

Уж я тоску́ю, пре́жней стра́сти по́лный,
uʃ ja taskuju prjɛʒnjɛi strastji pɔlnɨ

Свою́ свобо́ду вновь тебе́ отда́м
svaju svabɔdu vnɔfj tjɪbjɛ ad:dam

И уж бегу́т обра́тно с шу́мом во́лны
i uʃ bjigut abratna sʃumam vɔlnɨ

Издалека́ к люби́мым берега́м.
izdaljɪka kljubjimɨm bjɪrjɪgam

CD2  spoken text
piano accompaniment

Не верь, мой друг

Believe it not, my friend

Alexei Tolstoy
(1817–75)

Pyotr Ilyich Tchaikovsky Op. 6 No. 1
(1840–93)

Moderato assai [♩ = 68]

Original key

njɛ___ vjɛrj, mɔi druk, njɛ___ vjɛrj,_____ kag-dɑ ʃpɑ-
Not believe, my friend, not believe, when in outburst
Не___ верь, мой друг, не___ верь,_____ ког-да в по-

-rɪ___ vjɛ gɔ___rja ja ga-va-rju, ʃtɔ raz-lju-bjil tjɪ-bjɑ, v at-
(of) grief I say, that I–ceased–loving you, in low–tide
-ры___ ве го___ря Я го-во-рю, что раз-лю-бил те-бя, В от-

120

Нам звёзды кроткие сияли

The stars looked tenderly upon us　　　Pyotr Ilyich Tchaikovsky (1840–93) Op. 60 No. 12

Background

By August 1886, Tchaikovsky was living in Maidanovo and working on a new opera entitled *The Enchantress*. As ever, he was struggling with bouts of depression and a waning creative drive, but the arrival of some friends, and a particular request from the Empress Maria Fyodorovna to dedicate a romance to her, led to a burst of composition and ten of the final twelve Romances of Opus 60 were written. The Empress was apparently delighted with his gift of the set and responded in turn by sending him a signed portrait. The text by Alexei Pleshcheyev is on a familiar theme of Tchaikovsky's: the loss of love through the forces of fate or destiny. Pleshcheyev was a translator and one of the exponents of 19th century Russian 'civic poetry' – a movement that was concerned to express the politics and social conditions of ordinary peasant people. He had known Tchaikovsky in Moscow and the composer had earlier set the poet's collection of children's poems *The Snowdrop* to music in his Op. 54 *Children's Songs*.

Idiomatic translation

The stars gently shone for us,
A slight breeze was softly blowing,
Fragrant flowers were around us,
And waves sweetly murmured
At our feet.

We were young, we loved,
And gazed into the distance with trust;
Optimistic dreams dwelled within us,
And for us, the blizzards of grey winter
Were not frightening.

Where are those radiant nights
With their fragrant beauty
And mysterious murmuring waves,
Enthusiastic hopes and visions,
Where is that bright multitude?

The stars have faded, and the
Pale flowers have wilted …
When will you forget, oh heart,
Everything that used to be,
All that Spring gave us?

Pronunciation – **Нам звёзды кроткие сияли** [nɑm zvjɔzdɨ krɔtkjijɛ sjijɑlji]

Нам звёзды кро́ткие сия́ли,
nɑm zvjɔzdɨ krɔtkjijɛ sjijɑlji

Чуть ве́ял ти́хий ветеро́к,
tʃutj vjɛjal tjixji vjɪtjɪrɔk

Круго́м цветы́ благоуха́ли,
krugɔm tsvjɪtɨ blagauxɑlji

И во́лны ла́сково журча́ли
i vɔlnɨ lɑskava ʒurtʃɑlji

У на́ших ног.
u nɑʃix nɔk

Мы бы́ли ю́ны, мы люби́ли,
mɨ bɨlji junɨ mɨ ljubjɪlji

И с мело в даль смотре́ли мы;
i smjɛla vdalj smatrjɛlji mɨ

В нас грёзы ра́дужные жи́ли,
vnas grjɔzɨ rɑduʒnijɛ ʒɨlji

И нам не стра́шны вью́ги бы́ли
i nam nji strɑʃnɨ vjugji bɨlji

Седо́й зимы́.
sjidɔi zjimɨ

Где ж э́ти но́чи с их сия́ньем,
gdjɛʒ ɛtji nɔtʃi six sjijɑnjim

С благоуха́ющей красо́й
sblagauxɑjuʃtʃɛi krasɔi

И волн таи́нственным журча́ньем,
i vɔln tɑinstvjin:nɨm ʒurtʃɑnjim

Наде́жд, восто́рженных мечта́ний,
nadjɛzt vastɔrʒɛn:nix mjɪtʃtɑnji

Где све́тлый рой?
gdjɛ svjɛtlɨ rɔi

Поме́ркли звёзды, и уны́ло
pamjɛrklji zvjɔzdɨ i unɨla

Пони́кли бле́клые цветы́ …
panjiklji blɛklijɛ tsvjɪtɨ

Когда́ ж, о се́рдце, всё, что бы́ло,
kagdɑʃ ɔ sjɛrtsɛ fsjɔ ʃtɔ bɨla

Что нам весна́ с тобо́й дари́ла,
ʃtɔ nam vjɪsnɑ stabɔi dɑrjila

Забу́дешь ты?
zabudjɪʃ tɨ

CD2 — spoken text / piano accompaniment

Нам звёзды кроткие сияли

The stars looked tenderly upon us

Alexei Pleshcheyev
(1825–93)

Pyotr Ilyich Tchaikovsky Op. 60 No. 12
(1840–93)

-tʃɑ - lji u nɑ-ʃix nɔk.
at our feet.
-ча - ли У на-ших ног.

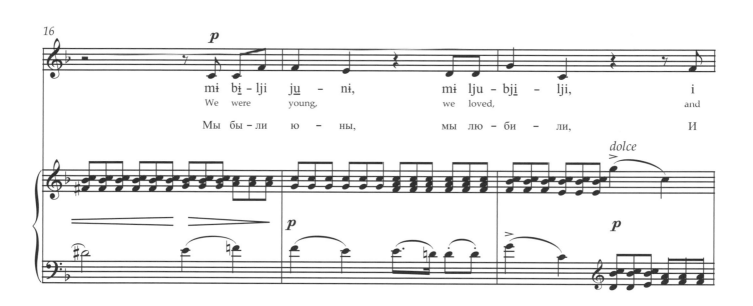

mɨ bɨ-lji ju - nɨ, mɨ lju-bjɪ - lji, i
We were young, we loved, and
Мы бы-ли ю - ны, мы лю-би - ли, И

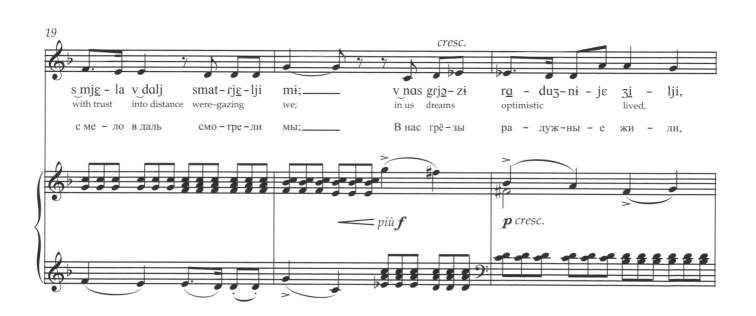

s mjɛ - la v dalj smat-rjɛ-lji mɨ; v nɑs grjɔ-zɨ rɑ - duʒ-nɨ - jɛ ʒɨ - lji,
with trust into distance were–gazing we; in us dreams optimistic lived,
с ме - ло в даль смо-тре-ли мы; В нас грё-зы ра - дуж-ны - е жи - ли,

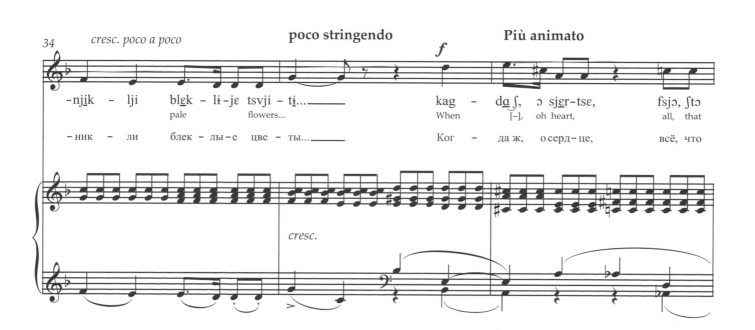

Весенние воды

Spring waters

Sergei Rachmaninov (1873–1943) Op. 14 No. 11

Background

Rachmaninov was born in Semyonovo, Russia. His parents' marriage and finances were unstable, and, having failed all his exams at the St Petersburg Conservatory due to family troubles, he was sent to the Moscow Conservatory at the age of twelve, where he lived with his piano teacher Zverev. In Moscow he met Rubenstein, Arensky and Tchaikovsky and he began to compose when he was fifteen. He is probably best remembered for his piano Prelude in C# minor and his Piano Concerto No. 2, but he also wrote operas (*Aleko*, *The Miserly Knight* and *Francesca da Rimini*), choral music (*The Bells*), orchestral music and chamber music. Rachmaninov's songs (over eighty of them) were written up until 1917 when, due to the political upheavals in Russia, Rachmaninov took his family to New York and thereafter claimed that he had lost the inspiration to write any more. They finally settled in Los Angeles, where he died of a cancer-related illness. 'Spring waters' is one of his most popular songs, written in 1896 and dedicated to his first piano teacher, Anna Ornatskaya. Its tumultuous piano accompaniment evokes the sounds of the Russian winter thaw and is set to a text by one of the last of the great Romantic Russian poets, Fyodor Tyutchev.

Idiomatic translation

The fields are still white with snow.
But the waters already babble with spring,
Rushing and awakening the sleepy shore,
Rushing and sparkling and proclaiming.

They are proclaiming to every quarter:
"Spring is coming, Spring is coming!
We are the heralds of young Spring,
She has sent us ahead,

Spring is coming, Spring is coming!"
And the peaceful, warm May days
In a rosy, bright roundelay,
Throng joyfully in the wake of spring.

Pronunciation – **Весéнние воды** [vjisjɛn:njija vɔdɨ]

Ещё в полях белéет снег,
jɪʃtʃɔ   fpaljɑx bjɪljɛjɛt snjɛk

А воды уж весной шумят,
a vɔdɨ uʃ vjɪsnɔi ʃumjɑt

Бегýт и бýдят сонный брег,
bjɪgut i bﻉudjat sɔn:nɨ brjɛk

Бегýт и блещут, и гласят.
bjɪgut i bljɛʃtʃut i glasjɑt

Они гласят во все концы́:
anji glasjɑt va fsjɛ kɑntsɨ

"Весна идёт, Весна идёт!
vjɪsnɑ idjɔt vjɪsnɑ idjɔt

Мы молодой весны гонцы́,
mɨ maladɔi vjɪsnɨ gɑntsɨ

Она нас вы́слала вперёд.
anɑ nɑs vɨslala fpjɪrjɔt

Весна идёт, Весна идёт!"
vjɪsnɑ idjɔt vjɪsnɑ idjɔt

И тихих, тёплых майских дней
i tjɪxjix tjɔpljɨx mɑiskjix dnjɛi

Румяный, свéтлый хоровод
rumjɑnɨ svjɛtlɨ xaravɔt

Толпится вéсело за ней.
talpjɪtsa vjɛsjɪla za njɛi

CD2 25 spoken text
26 piano accompaniment

Весенние воды

Spring waters

Fyodor Ivanovich Tyutchev
(1803–73)

Sergei Rachmaninov Op. 14 No. 11
(1873–1943)

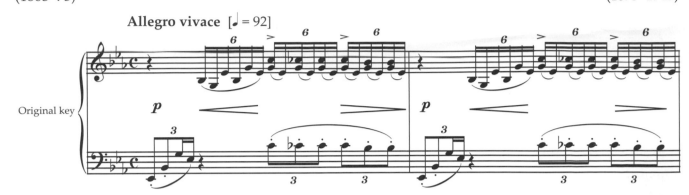

ji - ʃtʃɔ   f pa - ljɑx   bjɪ - ljɛ - jɛt   snjɛk,_____   ɑ
Still   in fields   whitens   snow,   and
Е - щё   в по-лях   бе - ле - ет   снег,_____   А

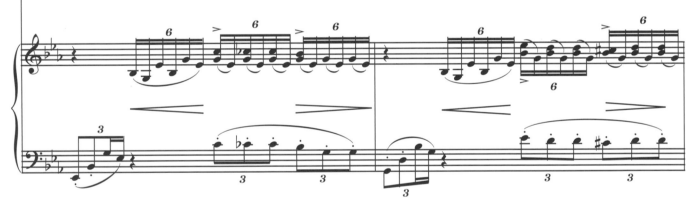

vɔ - di   uʃ   vjɪs - nɔi   ʃu - mjɑt,_____
waters   already (with) spring resound,
во - ды   уж   вес - ной   шу - мят,_____

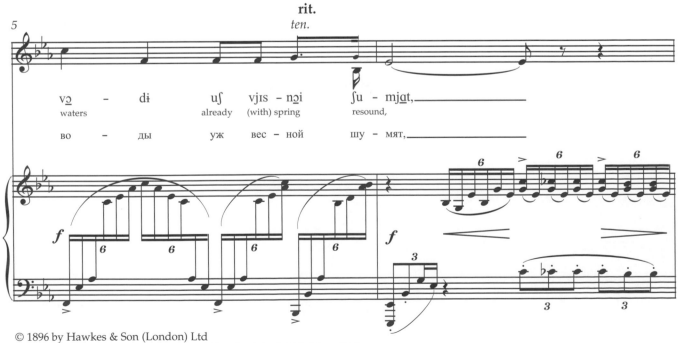

Key to International Phonetic Alphabet for Italian

Vowels	IPA	English sounds		Italian words
A	[a]	as in a bright 'ah'		caro [karɔ]
E	[ɛ]	open as in 'b_e_d'		bella [bɛl:la]
	[e]	close (prepare your tongue as if to say 'ee' and say 'ay' without dropping the jaw)		che [ke]
I	[i]	as in 'see' or 'pol_i_ce'		mi [mi], ti [ti]
O	[o]	close (say 'oh' with lips in a well-rounded position, jaw slightly dropped and no diphthong)		dolce [doltʃe]
	[ɔ]	open as in 'h_o_t'		bocca [bɔk:ka]
U	[u]	as in 'f_oo_d' or 'r_u_de'		tu [tu]

(Check the pronunciation guides carefully for open and closed vowels as Italian spelling does not differentiate these sounds.)
Note: There are no diphthongs in Italian – the vowels are often liaised but nevertheless are clearly delineated.

Semi-vowels

	[j]	as in 'yard'	piacer [pjatʃer]
	[w]	as in 'water'	acqua [ak:kwa]

Consonants

B, F, M and V are pronounced as in English.
D, N, T and L are pronounced as in English but with the tip of the tongue in a forward position, just behind the upper front teeth.

C	[tʃ]	as in 'church'	*before e or i*	ciel [tʃel], dicesti [ditʃesti]
C	[k]	as in 'cook'	*before a, o or u*	cor [kɔr]
SC	[ʃ]	as in 'shoe'	*before e or i*	scena [ʃena]
SC	[sk]	as in 'skull'		schiudi [skjudi], scherzo [skertsɔ]
G	[dʒ]	as in 'jar'	*before e or i*	giro [dʒirɔ], dipinge [dipindʒe]
G	[g]	as in 'good'		largo [largɔ], goder [goder]
P	[p]	as in 'pull'		pace [patʃe]
QU	[kw]	as in 'quick'		quel [kwel]
R	[ɾ]	slightly flipped 'r'	*between two vowels*	caro [karɔ]
R	[r]	trilled/rolled 'r'		ritardando [ritardandɔ]
S	[s]	as in 'so'		subito [subitɔ]
S	[z]	as in 'zoo'		rosa [roza]
Z	[ts]	as in 'pets'		grazia [grat:tsja], sembianze [sembjantse]
Z	[dz]	as in 'adds'		mezzo [med:dzɔ]

Extra notes

-GLI-	[ʎ]	like 'million'	*(the g is silent)*	voglio [vɔʎɔ]
-GN-	[ɲ]	like 'new' (ny-oo)	*(the g is silent)*	segno [seɲɔ]
-NG-	[ng]	Try to avoid the English 'ng' sound as in 'bring'. When singing, the 'n' may still be formed as above.		vengo [vengɔ]
H		is always silent		hanno [an:nɔ]
H		hardens C, G and SC		chi [ki], schiudi [skjudi]
I		is silent when used to soften C, G, or SC		già [dʒa], lascia [laʃa]

Double consonants

All double consonants should be emphasized with a slight 'stop' of the vowel before them – as in oggetto [ɔd:ʒet:tɔ], mattinata [mat:tinata].
A single **r** is lightly flipped. A double **rr** is strongly rolled.

Word endings

When singing in Italian, final vowels (unless marked with an accent eg: più [pju]) should never be stressed.

Key to International Phonetic Alphabet for German

Vowels	IPA	English sounds	German words
A	[aː]	long – as in 'far'	Vater [faːtə]
	[a]	short – as in 'undo'	Mann [man]
E	[eː]	long – no direct English equivalent but exactly the same as French é (prepare your tongue as if to say 'ee' and say 'ay' without dropping the jaw)	lebe [leːbə]
	[ɛ]	short – as in 'bed' or 'set'	denn [dɛn]
	[ə]	neutral – as in 'the' or 'again'	deine [dainə]
I	[iː]	long – as in 'see' or 'police'	die [diː], ihm [|iːm]
	[ɪ]	short – as in 'sit' or 'bin'	im [|ɪm], ich [|ɪç]
O	[oː]	long (say 'oh' with lips almost as closed as if for 'ooh' and with no diphthong)	Wohnung [voːnʊŋ]
	[ɔ]	short – as in 'hot'	kommt [kɔmt]
U	[uː]	long – as in 'food' or 'rude'	du [duː], Ruh [ruː]
	[ʊ]	short – as in 'put' or 'book'	und [|ʊnt], um [|ʊm]

Modified vowels

ä	[ɛː]	long – as in 'gate'	Tränen [trɛːnən]
	[ɛ]	short – as in 'bed' or 'set'	Hände [hɛndə]
ö	[œ]	short – the same sound as 'earth' but shorter	Hölle [hœlə]
	[øː]	long – as above but with lips more closed (the same as French 'deux')	schöne [ʃøːnə]
ü	[yː]	long (say 'ee' with closed lips in an 'oo' shape)	über [yːbɐ], Frühling [fryːlɪŋ]
	[ʏ]	short (try saying 'it' with closed lips in an 'oo' shape)	drücket [drʏkət]

Dipthongs

ai, ei	[ai]	as in 'aisle' or 'height'	Mai [mai], mein [main]
au	[au]	as in 'house' or 'flower'	Auge [|augə], Frau [frau]
äu, eu	[ɔi]	as in 'boy' or 'oil'	Äuglein [|ɔiglain], neu [nɔi]

As in English, when singing a diphthong, spend most time on the first of the combined vowels, leaving the second to the last moment before finishing the word or syllable.

Glottal stop [|]

The slight stopping of the breath and starting the sound (as in 'umbrella') takes place in German before any word beginning with a vowel. The intensity of this is open to artistic interpretation, but it should never be overdone or create any danger of injuring the voice.

Consonants

Consonants are pronounced as in English with the following exceptions:

g is always pronounced hard as in 'good' (*but see* '**Endings**' *below*)	Glanz [glants]
h is silent after a vowel, otherwise it is aspirated	Sohn [zoːn] Herz [hɛrts]
j is pronounced as an English 'y' as in 'yes'	ja [jaː]
k is pronounced before 'n' (it is never silent)	Knabe [knaːbə]
r is slightly 'flipped' [ɾ] before a consonant	Herz [hɛrts], sterben [ʃtɛrbən]
r is rolled [r] at the beginning of word or after another consonant	Rose [rozə] Grab [grap]
s before vowels, as in English 'z' (*but see below*)	sein [zain] Rose [rozə]
v mostly as in English 'f'	voll [fɔl]
w as in English 'v'	wenn [vɛn]
z as in 'cats'	zum [tsʊm] Schmerz [ʃmɛrts]

Double consonants and other sounds

Vowels	IPA	English sounds	German words
ck	[k]	as in 'lock'	Blick [blɪk]
ch	[x]	after **a, o, u** and **au** – closest to Scottish 'loch' (place tongue in the position for 'k' and say 'h')	doch [dɔx], nach [nax]
ch	[ç]	after **e, i, ä, eu** or a consonant as in (whispered) 'yes' (place tongue in the position for 'ee' and say 'h')	ich [ǀɪç], durch [dʊrç]
ph	[f]	as in 'telephone'	Phantasie [fantazi:]
pf	[pf]	both letters sounded	Pforten [pfɔrtən]
qu	[kv]	sounds like English 'kv...'	Qual [kva:l]
ß	[s]	as in 'kiss'	laß [las]
sch	[ʃ]	as in English 'ship'	schöne [ʃø:nə]
sp, st	[ʃp, ʃt]	sounds like English 'sht' or 'shp' *(at the beginning of a word, or after a prefix)*	Spiel [ʃpi:l], still [ʃtɪl] erstanden [ǀɛɐʃtandən]
-ng	[ŋ]	as in 'sing'	kling [klɪŋ]

Note: Unlike Italian, where double consonants are marked, in German they are treated as single consonants unless the need to express the word more imaginatively leads to emphasizing them (this is equally true of single consonants).

Endings of words/prefixes/word elements

	IPA		
-er	[ɐ]	as in 'sister'	guter [gu:tɐ]
-r	[ɐ]	usually not pronounced (but check IPA in songs for exceptions)	nur [nu:ɐ], vor [fo:ɐ]
-en	[ən]	as in 'garden'	meinen [mainən]
b		at the end of a word sounds 'p'	Grab [grap]
d		at the end of a word sounds 't'	Lied [li:t], und [ǀʊnt]
s		at the end of a word as in 'less'	liebes [li:bəs], dies [di:s]
g		at the end of a word sounds 'k'	Sonntag [zɔnta:k]
-ig	[ɪç]	as in the German word 'ich'	ewig [ǀeviç]

General note

Even though there are many consonants in German, the legato line (as in all singing) is still paramount and consonants need to be quick and crisp.

Key to International Phonetic Alphabet for French

Vowels	IPA	English sounds		French words
a	[ɑ]	long – as in 'far'		âme [ɑmə]
	[a]	short – as in a bright 'ah'		la, [la], amour [amuʀ]
e	[e]	long (prepare your tongue as if to say 'ee' and say 'ay' without dropping the jaw)		été [ete], et [e]
	[ɛ]	short – as in 'bed' or 'set'		est [ɛ], belle [bɛlə]
	[ə]	neutral – as in 'the'		le [lə], que [kə]
i	[i]	long – as in 'see' or 'police'		si [si], qui [ki]
o	[o]	long (say 'oh' with lips in a well-rounded position, jaw slightly dropped and no diphthong)		rose [ʀozə], vos [vo]
	[ɔ]	short – as in 'hot'		comme [kɔmə]
u	[y]	long (say 'ee' with well-rounded lips in an 'oo' shape)		tu [ty], une [ynə]
ou	[u]	long – as in 'food' or 'rude'		tous [tus], pour [puʀ]
eu	[œ]	open (say 'earth' and drop the jaw)		leur [lœʀ], cœur [kœʀ]
	[ø]	closed (as above but with lips well-rounded)		deux [dø], feu [fø]

Nasalized vowels

[ɑ̃]	long [ɑ] (far) nasalized		blanc [blɑ̃], semble [sɑ̃blə]
[ɛ̃]	short [æ] (fat) nasalized		matin [matɛ̃], essaim [esɛ̃]
[õ]	long [o] (oh) nasalized		mon [mõ], ombre [õbʀə]
[œ̃]	short [œ] (the) nasalized		un [œ̃], parfum, [paʀfœ̃]

Although nasal vowels are always followed by an -n or -m in the spelling, these consonants are **not** pronounced either in speech or in singing unless they form a liaison with a word beginning with a vowel.

Semi-vowels

[j]	using an English 'y' sound, as in 'piano'	bien [bjɛ̃], ciel [sjɛl]
[w]	as in 'quack'	moi [mwa], voyant [vwajɑ̃]
[ɥ]	Try to say the 'y' in 'une' very quickly before the 'i'. It should not sound like a 'w'.	lui [lɥi], nuit [nɥi]

Consonants

b d f k l m n p t v w y x z

The above consonants are pronounced as in English, though in French (as in Italian) there is no explosion of breath with **p, t, k**. Also, double consonants are not marked and are spoken or sung as if single.

c	[k]	hard as in 'cook'	*before a,o,u/ending words*	comme [kɔmə], lac [lak]
c/ç	[s]	soft as in 'piece'	*c-before e, i/ç- before a, u, o*	ce [sə], français [fʀɑ̃sɛ]
g	[g]	hard as in 'good'	*before a, o, u*	gauche [goʃə]
	[ʒ]	soft as in 'pleasure'	*before e, i*	age [aʒə]
h		is usually silent		hélas [‖elas]
j	[ʒ]	is pronounced as in 'pleasure'		je [ʒə], jardin [ʒaʀdɛ̃]
l	[l]	like an Italian 'forward' 'l' (soft and quick) *(but also sometimes silent)*		lune [lynə], gentil [ʒɑ̃ti]
qu	[k]	pronounced as a 'k' and without the 'w'		que, [kə] qui [ki]
r	[ʀ]	uvula is vibrated by a vocalised breath against the back of the tongue (see note below)		rien [ʀiɛ̃]
s	[s]	unvoiced as in 'so'		sur [syʀ]
	[z]	voiced as in 'gaze'	*between two vowels*	rosée [rozeə]
x	[ks]	as in 'example'		extase [ɛkstɑzə]
	[gs]	as in 'eggs'		examiner [ɛgzamine]
	[z]		*in a liaison*	deux_amis [dø(z)ami]
		silent as a final consonant	*no liaison*	deux [dø], yeux [jø]

Other sounds

Vowels	IPA	English sounds		French words
-ai	[e]	closed 'e' at the end of a word		aimerai [ɛməʀe]
-ais/-ait/-aient	[ɛ]	open 'e' at the end of a word (verb endings)		mais [mɛ], avaient [avɛ]
-au/-eau	[o]	long (say 'oh' with lips in a well-rounded position, jaw slightly dropped and no diphthong)		beau [bo]
ch	[ʃ]	as in 'shoe'		chanter [ʃɑ̃te]
-ail	[aj]	as in English 'eye' (with a pronounced 'y')		travail [travaj]
-eil	[ɛj]	as in English 'eh' followed by 'y'		sommeil [sɔmɛj]
-euil/oeil	[œj]	as in English 'err' followed by 'y'		feuille [fœj], oeil [œj]
-ouille	[uj]	as in English 'ooh' followed by 'y'		mouiller [muje]
-ille/quille	[ilə]	as in 'elongate'		ville [vilə], tranquille [tʀɑ̃kilə]
-er/ez	[e]		as a word ending	monter [mɔ̃te], assez [ase]
-gn-	[ɲ]	as in 'onion'		ligne [liɲə]
ph	[f]	as in 'telephone'		séraphin [seʀafɛ̃]
th	[t]	pronounced as a 't'		théatre [teatʀə]

Word endings

A final -e, -es and the verb ending -ent are silent in speech, but in singing are often given a note. These are sung to the neutral [ə] vowel but should never be emphasized; phrase them off tastefully wherever possible.

Liaisons

The decision whether or not to join the final consonant (or consonant plus [ə]) to a following word beginning with a vowel is always a thorny one and the academic rules are complex. Contemporary tastes are always evolving and liaisons arc used increasingly less frequently. In this volume, the IPA liaisons should be executed gently and without too much emphasis.

Vocalic harmonisation

In French, vocalic harmonisation is the rhyming of closely related vowel sounds around adjoining syllables (either within one word or between two neighbouring words). It happens with only two pairs of vowels: between [ɛ] and [e] and between [ə] and [ø], and occurs when one of these open vowels is followed by its closed counterpart and the open vowel closes to rhyme with it. It does not work the other way round. Thus *baiser* [bɛze] and *cheveux* [ʃəvø] become [beze] and [ʃøvø], and *les étoiles* [lɛ(z)etwalə] becomes [lez(e)twalə]. This occurs in speech but cannot be assumed in every case in singing and is open to artistic interpretation. Check the IPA guide carefully for each song and listen to the CD for any suggested vocalic harmonisation.

Rolling the 'r' in French

In classical singing, it has been considered good taste to pronounce the rolled 'r' in the Italian style (i.e. with the tip of the tongue in a forward position). Contemporary tastes, however, seem to be moving towards the traditional uvular 'r', even in classical song and opera. In this guide, we recommend the uvular 'r' [ʀ]. In French Baroque repertoire, however, a rolled Italian 'r' [r] would still be considered stylistic.

Key to International Phonetic Alphabet for Russian

Phonetics or transliteration

Note that in this edition and in keeping with the principles of *The Language of Song* series, we have used a phonetic system to show Russian sounds, rather than a transliteration. Therefore, some sounds are represented with different symbols. Study this simple key to familiarise yourself with the Russian sounds.

This system has been simplified to offer a basic pronunciation of the language. For a more comprehensive and thorough explanation of the rules of Russian pronunciation, see *Russian Songs and Arias* by Jean Piatak and Regina Avrashov (published 1991, Caldwell Publishing Co).

Vowels

There are 'hard' and 'soft' vowels and consonants in Russian. The vowel governs the preceding consonant. Therefore, if the vowel is 'soft', the preceding consonant will be correspondingly 'soft' and if the vowel is 'hard', the preceding consonant is 'hard'.

Vowels	IPA	English sounds		Russian words
(Hard)				
А а	[ɑ]	as in 'far'		как [kɑk], давнó [dɑvnɔ]
Э э	[ɛ]	as in 'bed'		это [ɛtɑ]
Ы ы	[ɨ]	prepare to say 'ü' [y:] but say 'ee' [i] in a guttural position		вы [vɨ]
О о	[ɔ]	as in 'hot'		вóпли [vɔplji]
У у	[u]	as in 'food' or 'rude'		скýчно [skuʃna]
(Soft)				
Я я	[jɑ]	as in 'yard'		явка [jɑfka]
Е е	[jɛ]	as in 'yes'		едет [jɛdɪt]
И и	[i]	as in 'see'		ива [ivɑ]
Й й	[i]	as in 'toy'	*(the end of a diphthong)*	той [tɔi]
Ё ё	[jɔ]	as in 'yore'		ёлка [jɔlkɑ]
Ю ю	[ju]	as in 'you'		юность [junastj]

Note: In Russian, vowel pronunciation can change depending on the stress of words (marked above the Cyrillic letter with an accent [']), or the consonants used.

О	can become [ɑ] *see above* or [a] as in 'undo'	собóй [sabɔi], поля́х [paljɑx]
Е е	can become [ɛ] *see above* or [ɪ] as in 'sit'	цветок [tsvjɪtɔk]
Я я	can become [jɪ], or [ja]	яровá [jɪravɑ], явить [jɪvitj]
		горя [gɔrja]

There are three exceptions where the consonant governs the vowel. After **Ж, Ш** and **Ц**, the vowel is always hard; for example, in the word **живá** [ʒɨvɑ], the **И** [i] is hardened to a [ɨ] sound. Listen to the CD and follow the phonetics carefully.

Consonants

In the chart below, the softening of the consonants is represented most closely by the 'y' [j] sound. This should, however, be executed very lightly, as a passing sound only.

	(hard)		(soft)			(hard)		(soft)	
Б б	[b]	body	[bj]	beauty	П п	[p]	pop	[pj]	pew
Д д	[d]	day	[dj]	dew	Р р	[r]	'rolled'	[rj]	'flipped' in
Ф ф	[f]	far	[fj]	few					'soft' position
Г г	[g]	game	[gj]	argue	С с	[s]	sad	[sj]	assume
К к	[k]	cat	[kj]	cue	Т т	[t]	talk	[tj]	costume
Л л	[l]	hull	[lj]	million *(or Ital. 'gli')*	В в	[v]	voice	[vj]	view
М м	[m]	man	[mj]	music	Х х	[x]	German 'ach'	[xj]	no equivalent
Н н	[n]	net	[nj]	new	З з	[z]	zoo	[zj]	resume

Double consonants

Double consonants in Russian are treated in a similar way to Italian double consonants. They are shown in phonetics by a lengthening symbol [ː] and should be emphasized by a slight 'stop' on the sound, e.g.: **отдаленной** [adːdaljɛnːnɑi].

Other sounds

Ж ж	(hard)	[ʒ]	as in 'plea<u>s</u>ure'	жар [ʒɑr]
Ц ц	(hard)	[ts]	as in 'ca<u>ts</u>' or '<u>ts</u>ar'	царь [tsɑrj]
Ч ч	(soft)	[tʃ]	as in '<u>ch</u>ur<u>ch</u>'	час [tʃas]
Ш ш	(hard)	[ʃ]	as in '<u>sh</u>oe'	шум [ʃum]
Щ щ	(soft)	[ʃtʃ]	as in 'pu<u>shch</u>air'	прощай [praʃtʃɑi]

The symbols Ъ and Ь

These symbols do not have sounds of their own but are very important in Russian spelling as they affect the sound of the preceding consonants.

Ъ ъ	hardens a preceding consonant	объятия [abjɑtjija]
Ь ь	softens a preceding consonant	больной [baljnɔi]

Voiced and voiceless consonant sounds

Some voiced consonants can be pronounced as their voiceless equivalents. Final consonants are often voiceless. Be aware of the following consonant pairs but follow the phonetics and CD carefully.

voiced	voiceless
б [b]	п [p]
в [v]	ф [f]
г [g]	к [k]
д [d]	т [t]
ж [ʒ]	ш [ʃ]
з [z]	с [s]

New and Old Russian

In 1918, a new decree on orthography abolished the letters i, ѣ and ѳ in Russian and replaced them with **и, е** or (**ё**), and **ф**. In this edition, we have used the new Russian Cyrillic alphabet throughout.

Also available in the Language of Song series

ELEMENTARY
High Voice & Low Voice

INTERMEDIATE
High Voice & Low Voice

ISBN10: 0-571-52345-5
ELEMENTARY HIGH

ISBN10: 0-571-52346-3
ELEMENTARY LOW

ISBN10: 0-571-52343-9
INTERMEDIATE HIGH

ISBN10: 0-571-52344-7
INTERMEDIATE LOW

Contents

Caro mio ben • Tommaso Giordani

Santa Lucia • Teodoro Cottrau

Non lo dirò col labbro • Georg Frideric Handel

Sebben, crudele • Antonio Caldara

Nina • Anonymous

Alma del core • Antonio Caldara

Nel cor più non mi sento • Giovanni Paisiello

Vittoria, mio core! • Giacomo Carissimi

Gruß • Felix Mendelssohn

An die Laute • Franz Schubert

Kinderwacht • Robert Schumann

Frühlingslied • Franz Schubert

Wiegenlied • Johannes Brahms

Sonntag • Johannes Brahms

Heidenröslein • Franz Schubert

Dein blaues Auge • Johannes Brahms

Chevaliers de la table ronde • French folksong

Bois épais • Jean-Baptiste Lully

En prière • Gabriel Fauré

Lydia • Gabriel Fauré

Contents

Tu lo sai • Giuseppe Torelli

Toglietemi la vita ancor • Alessandro Scarlatti

Amarilli, mia bella • Giulio Caccini

Se tu m/ami • *attr.* Alessandro Parisotti

Vaga luna • Vincenzo Bellini

An Chloë • Wolfgang Amadeus Mozart

Vergebliches Ständchen • Johannes Brahms

Ständchen • Franz Schubert

Mariä Wiegenlied • Max Reger

Die Lotosblume • Robert Schumann

Die Forelle • Franz Schubert

Le charme • Ernest Chausson

Le secret • Gabriel Fauré

Aurore • Gabriel Fauré

Clair de lune • Gabriel Fauré

El majo discreto • Enrique Granados

En Jerez de la Frontera • Joaquín Rodrigo

Canción de cuna • Xavier Montsalvatge